Complete Plus

Other publications by George Economou

Poetry
The Georgics
Landed Natures
Poems for Self-Therapy
Ameriki; Book One and Selected Earlier Poems
Voluntaries
harmonies & fits
Century Dead Center
Ananios of Kleitor

Translations
Philodemos, His Twenty-Nine Extant Poems
William Langland's Piers Plowman, A Verse Translation of the C Version
I've Gazed So Much, Poems by C. P. Cavafy
Acts of Love, Ancient Greek Poetry from Aphrodite's Garden
Half an Hour, Poems by C. P. Cavafy

Criticism
The Goddess Natura in Medieval Literature
Janus Witness: Testament of a Greek American Poet

Editor
Geoffrey Chaucer, A Collection of Original Articles
In Pursuit of Perfection: Courtly Love in Medieval Literature, with Joan M. Ferrante
Proensa, An Anthology of Troubadour Poetry Translated by Paul Blackburn
Poem of the Cid, translated by Paul Blackburn

Complete Plus

The Poems of C.P. Cavafy in English

translated by
George Economou
with
Stavros Deligiorgis

Shearsman Books

First published in the United Kingdom in 2013 by
Shearsman Books
50 Westons Hill Drive
Emersons Green
BRISTOL
BS16 7DF

Shearsman Books Ltd Registered Office
30–31 St. James Place, Mangotsfield, Bristol BS16 9JB
(this address not for correspondence)

www.shearsman.com

ISBN 978-1-84861-266-2

Translations, Introduction and 'Pantoum for C. P. Cavafy and a Translator'
copyright © George Economou, 2013.

The right of George Economou to be identified as the translator
of this work has been asserted by him in accordance with the
Copyrights, Designs and Patents Act of 1988.
All rights reserved.

Acknowledgements
Grateful acknowledgement is made to the Stop Press of London, which published
two books, *I've Gazed So Much* and *Half an Hour*, in which forty-three of the
translations in this book previously appeared. A few of those translations
have been slightly revised.

Several of the translations in this book have appeared in the following publications:
American Poetry Review, Asymptote, Calque, Literary Matters,
and *Mediterranean Poetry*.

Credit for the following translations and original poem by George Economou in
this book's introduction belongs to *Acts of Love, Ancient Greek Poetry from Aphrodite's
Garden* (New York: Modern Library, Random House, 2006), for all translations
from *The Greek Anthology*; *Asymptote*, for the translation of the fragment by
Archilochos; *Jacket 2* and *Poems and Poetics* for 'The Newspaper Story.'

The cover design of this book makes use of a detail from a 1929 photograph
of C. P. Cavafy, which is be found in the Cavafy Archive.

Contents

Introduction	11
Ode and Elegy of the Street	31
Walls	32
An Old Man	33
Achilles' Horses	34
Prayer	35
Sarpedon's Funeral	36
Candles	38
The First Step	39
The Souls of Old Men	40
Che Fece… Il Gran Rifuto	41
Interruption	42
The Windows	43
Thermopylae	44
Perfidy	45
Waiting for the Barbarians	47
Voices	49
Desires	50
On the Stairs	51
In the Theater	52
Trojans	53
King Demetrius	54
The Retinue of Dionysus	55
Monotony	56
Hidden Things	57
The Footsteps	58
He's the Man	59
The City	60
The Satrapy	61
The Ides of March	62
Finished	63
Sculptor from Tyana	64
The God Abandons Antony	65
Ionic	66

The Glory of the Ptolemies	67
Ithaca	68
Dangerous Matters	70
Philhellene	71
Herodes Atticus	72
Alexandrian Kings	73
Return	75
In Church	76
Very seldom	77
As Much As You Can	78
For the Shop	79
I Went	80
Tomb of Lysias the Grammarian	81
Tomb of Eurion	82
Chandelier	83
Far Away	84
Returning Home from Greece	85
But Wise Men Apprehend What Is Imminent	86
Theodotus	87
At the Café Door	88
He Swears	89
One Night	90
Morning Sea	91
Painted	92
Orophernes	93
The Battle of Magnesia	95
Manuel Comnenus	96
The Displeasure of the Seleucid	97
When They Stir in Your Mind	98
In the Street	99
Facing the Statue of Endymion	100
In a Town of Osroene	101
Passage	102
For Ammonis, Who Died at 29 in 610	103
One of their Gods	104
In the Evening	105
To Pleasure	106

Gray	107
Tomb of Iases	108
In the Month of Athyr	109
I've Gazed So Much	110
Tomb of Ignatius	111
Days of 1903	112
The Tobacco Shop Window	113
Half an Hour	114
Symeon	115
Caesarion	116
Remember, Body	117
Tomb of Lanes	118
Getting It	119
Nero's Deadline	120
Envoys from Alexandria	121
Aristoboulus	122
In the Harbor	124
Aemilianus Monae, Alexandrian, A.D. 628-655	125
Since Nine O'Clock	126
Below the House	127
The Next Table	128
The Afternoon Sun	129
Comes to Reside	130
Of the Jews (50 A.D.)	131
Imenus	132
Aboard Ship	133
Of Demetrius Soter (162-150 B.C.)	134
The Bandaged Shoulder	136
If Dead Then	137
Young Men of Sidon (400 A.D.)	139
So They'll Come—	140
Darius	141
Anna Comnena	143
A Byzantine Noble, In Exile, Versifying	144
Their Beginning	145
The Favor of Alexander Valas	146

Melancholy of Jason Cleander,	
Poet in Commagene, 595 A.D.	147
Demaratus	148
I Brought to Art	150
From the School of the Renowned Philosopher	151
Craftsman of Wine Bowls	152
Those Who Fought for the Achaean League	153
To Antiochus Epiphanes	154
In an Antique Book	155
In Despair	156
Julian Seeing Indifference	157
Epitaph of Antiochus, King of Commagene	158
Theatre of Sidon (A.D. 400)	159
Julian in Nicomedia	160
Before Time Could Change Them	161
He Came to Read	162
31 B.C. in Alexandria	163
John Cantacuzenus Triumphs	164
Temethus, Antiochian: 400 A.D.	165
Of Colored Glass	166
In the Twenty-fifth Year of His Life	167
On an Italian Shore	168
In the Boring Village	169
Apollonius of Tyana in Rhodes	170
Kleitos' Illness	171
In a Township in Asia Minor	172
Priest at the Serapeum	173
In the Dives—	174
A Great Procession of Priests and Laymen	175
Sophist Leaving Syria	176
Julian and the Antiochians	177
Anna Dalassene	178
Days of 1896	179
Two Young Men, 23 to 24 Years Old	180
Greek Since Ancient Times	182
Days of 1901	183
You Didn't Understand	184

A Young Man, Devoted to the Art of the Word— in His Twenty-Fourth Year	185
In Sparta	186
Portrait of a Twenty-Three Year Old Painted by his Friend of the Same Age, an Amateur	187
In a Large Greek Colony, 200 B.C.	188
A Prince from Western Libya	190
Kimon, Son of Learchus, Age 22, Student of Greek Literature (in Cyrene)	191
On the March to Sinope	192
Days of 1909, '10, and '11	193
Myres: Alexandria, 340 A.D.	194
Alexander Jannaeus and Alexandra	197
Lovely White Flowers So Well-Suited	198
Come, O King of the Lacedaimonians	199
In the Same Space	200
The Mirror in the Vestibule	201
He Asked about the Quality	202
Should Have Taken Care	204
According to the Recipes of Ancient Greco-Syrian Magicians	206
In the Year 200 B.C.	207
Days of 1908	209
In the Outskirts of Antioch	211
Notes	214
Biographical Notes	226

Introduction

Translation should embody an act of thanks to the original. It should celebrate its own dependence on its source. It concentrates scruple and trust, however recreative or anarchic its instincts. It is an informing craft which, sometimes enigmatically, reveals within or adds to the original what was already there—particularly where the text has been translated, imitated, adapted a hundredfold.
—George Steiner

In the eighth of his *Twelve Poems for Cavafy* (*Dodeka Poiemata yia Kavafy*, 1974) entitled 'Misunderstandings,' the Greek poet Yiannis Ritsos assures his readers that the older, deceased Alexandrian poet is clearly out to entangle us in his singular complexity. By now, almost four decades later, this complexity, often conveyed through a poetic medium that seems on its surface relatively simple, defines and sustains his preeminent status among poets of the last one hundred and fifty years. Ritsos spoke of the man in order to speak of the poet, as if they are indissolubly bonded, just as we habitually do despite the hard fact of knowing the poet alone survives and succeeds the man. The complexity we share with Cavafy endures in the complexity of his poetry and our engagement with it.

That we know so very little about his life compared to those of many other poets of his own and other periods—Robert Liddell's slim 222-page *Cavafy: A Critical Biography* has occupied a lonely spot in the poet's bibliography for years—can neither be denied nor redressed by special narratives suited to persons of other times and places. A totally voiceless Cavafy, depicted in the 1996 biographical motion picture *Kavafis* by Yiannis Smaradgis, constitutes what is perhaps the most remarkable and memorable feature of the film. The character Cavafy throughout, from childhood to deathbed, says nothing, not a word. Even when one of the friends of his youth cries out in exasperation, "Ma yiati then milas; Pos mboris nase toso krifos;" (*So why don't you speak? How can you be so secretive?*) this cinematic Cavafy, symbolically true to his real life original, tells him and ultimately all of his fellow players nothing, though the words of the poet, tellingly, can be heard in the voice-over recitations of his poems in a number of scenes.

Although the biographical approach to Cavafy's poetry has been something of a dead-end, the bibliographical and textual focus on Cavafy's unique way of self-publishing his poems and on subsequent approaches to arranging and editing them has been a necessary and rewarding, if, at times, extravagant undertaking. The task of editing Cavafy's some 250 poems, comprising the 154 poems he collected and published himself during his lifetime, usually referred to as the *Collected* or *Published Poems*, and the two other groups of poems, the larger of which is categorized as *Uncollected* or *Unpublished*, never having been gathered and printed under the poet's living eye, and a number of early poems written between 1886 and 1898 that Cavafy "rejected," has demanded the unremitting attention of eminent scholars for the last several decades. Somewhat reminiscent of the editorial history of Emily Dickinson, the editing and publication history of Cavafy, primarily concerning the *Collected Poems*, has not been without some controversy, particularly on the issue of editorial intervention. As Anthony Hirst contends, "Cavafy left very little for subsequent editors to do. If only they had been content to do very little instead of undoing the poet's meticulous work!"

If in editing Cavafy scholars have managed to overlook some of his choices as self-editor, and thus some of his decisions as a writer as well, they have found much to say about his collecting and ordering poems in the seven thematically arranged publication packets for private circulation. Though every effort of scholarly criticism, just as every effort at translating the poetry, surely contributes something of value to our common enterprise, the fervent examination of these gatherings, at times pervaded with speculations about what guided Cavafy in assorting them, not to mention the search for clues to the meaning of individual poems consequent to these groupings, run the risk of over-privileging ongoing unstable contexts and of compartmentalizing his life's work after it was finished. Cavafy himself made a notable remark concerning these collections in a 1922 letter to a friend, "How can I speak for the future?" His pertinent question about this uncertainty, along with the fact that he also made five chronological gatherings, argue for preferment of the long view over continuing attention to such aspects of the poetry, which can also prove unproductive if driven by an impulse to compensate for the scant biographical material.

Let us pursue grounds more relative than this: the poetry's the thing. At the head of the 162 poems in this book, whose contents include the 154 *Collected Poems*, presented by the year and within each year's order of composition and/ or first printing, and seven of the *Uncollected Poems* interspersed chronologically among them, stands 'Ode and Elegy of the Street,' the only editorial choice here that infringes upon Cavafy's wishes to repudiate twenty-seven of his earliest poems. Conscripted as an overture to the story of Cavafy's poetry, 'Ode and Elegy of the Street' offers a portal through which we may enter the wide-open world of a young poet's receptivity to the possibilities before him. Between the opening and closing of the windows and doors in the morning and evening of his day, an extraordinary assembly of poems will eventually make its entrance, poems that will be disposed through a diversity of subjects and will take a lifetime of work to explore. It should not come as a surprise that in the first few pages that follow these introductory verses, the numerous poems to come that are rooted in Greek culture and history from antiquity to Byzantium are announced by 'Achilles' Horses,' 'Sarpedon's Funeral,' 'Thermoplyae,' and 'Perfidy.' The poems 'Prayer,' 'Candles,' 'An Old Man,' and 'The Souls of Old Men,' strike the elegiac notes of loss and regret that will be confronted and uniquely contested in the future, while 'Walls' and 'The Windows' represent the aura of self-imprisoning states of mind and social conditions from which there is no escape though there must some day be one. And the poem 'The First Step,' in describing the beginning of a commitment to art, foreshadows a lifelong progress from an intern on the first rung of poetry's ladder to a master with a consummate grasp of the empowerment of poetry and a dramatic command of a diversity of characters, historical, fictional, perhaps even personal through whom to give it voice.

Viewing the body of Cavafy's poems as a whole rather than continuing to speculate on the relevance of the thematic collections to his development as an artist, a fair though by now narrow interest of those still concerned with the contours of its progress rather than with its final state, we should attend to the poet's further remarks in the letter quoted above that the entire body of his work is not separated into "Special Collections" and that the earlier thematic arrangements had become subject to change. Thus, though when we look through the table of contents of almost any book of Cavafy poems we still recognize their fundamental organization around the familiar divisions of philosophical, historical, and erotic poems, we are also obliged to recognize and respond to the interpretive opportunities that other dynamics at work within those allocations present. One of these dynamics, which I call 'Eros, Memory, and Art,' originated in my 1981 review essay on Cavafy of that title in *The American Poetry Review*, coupled with Cavafy's own sense of himself as primarily a historical poet, helps to explain the unusual degree of overlapping of theme and approach that occurs throughout his *oeuvre*. One of the fundamental ways in which this works may be seen in 'Craftsman of Wine Bowls,' a poem linked to several others through a historical event, the Battle of Magnesia (190 B.C.) and its aftermath. While it is a common trait of many of Cavafy's historical poems to form a constellation of poems dealing with a single incident that has been carefully excised from history's seamless garment, the contextual parameters of some of them expand exponentially when viewed through the lens of Eros, Memory, and Art. Thus, a poem like 'Craftsman,' which begins by illustrating the combination of the personal and political, the private and public, spheres that frequently intersect in Cavafy's poetry, the artisan-speaker, working on commission by a great family, insinuates his individual celebration of his love as he simultaneously experiences the eroding effects of time upon his memory of that love. By dating his personal loss by the battle that marks the great political loss that came with the onset of Roman dominance in the Hellenized East, the craftsman-persona inadvertently unveils an ironic historical context that is more meaningful to the reader than to himself. Relative chronological proximity to the battle provides him with his poignancy, chronological distance provides the reader with his ironic perspective. One more step back from (or into?) this hall of mirrors kind of perspective, gives the final Cavafian twist, the proposal that the poet himself keeps company with his reader and his fictional artisan, that they are each and all participants in their own immediate situations that are subject to partially understood historical forces and full of passion and loss. Though pathetic, and often tragic, these situations have been intermittently dignified by art's attempt to record their intensity and sincerity.

Craftsman of Wine Bowls

On this wine bowl   of pure silver—
made for the house   of Herakleides,
where grand style   and good taste rule—
observe the elegant flowers,   streams and thyme,
in whose midst I set   a handsome young man,
naked, amorous,   with one leg still
dangling in the water.—   O memory, I prayed
you'd be my best assistant   in making
the young man's face I loved   the way it was.
A great difficulty   this proved because
about fifteen years   have passed since the day
he fell, a soldier,   in the defeat at Magnesia.

With its first version written in November of 1903, a revision in July 1912, and the final version and printing in December of 1921, 'Craftsman of Wine Bowls' significantly occupies stations across two richly creative decades of the poet's career. Coincidentally, in 1903 at the beginning of this formative period in which the first draft of 'Craftsman' was composed, Cavafy wrote an untitled work in English prose, now known as *Ars Poetica*, that was not published until 1963, thirty years after his death, in which he assayed his work and role as a poet. His remarks in the following passage about two of his early poems, written in the same period, suggest the kind of poetic thinking that might have helped inspire the dynamic that energizes 'Craftsman of Wine Bowls."

> If even for one day, or one hour I felt like the man within 'Walls,' or like the man of 'Windows' the poem is based on a truth, a short-lived truth, but which, for the very reason of its having once existed, may repeat itself in another life, perhaps with as short duration, perhaps with longer.

Notably, poems from this general period such as 'Comes to Reside,' 'Their Beginning,' 'Very Seldom,' 'Getting It,' and 'One Night' establish, each in its own way, the importance of the artist's role in the struggle to preserve love and the beloved against defacement "by Time's fell hand." Poems like these, dealing with the poet's desire to memorialize in his work an individual or experience, invariably recalled for their erotic significance and for which he cares deeply, launched the possibility for the extension and integration of Cavafy's perception of the relevance of Eros, Memory, and Art to poems that would be written in the years to come. In 1930-31, two years before he died, Cavafy composed and printed two poems that give supremely conceived and executed expression to this major creative force in his writing: 'The Mirror in the Vestibule,' with its consummately refined symbolic image of the poet as an eighty-year old mirror in the house of poetry proudly and joyfully reflecting the perfect beauty that appears, if only fleetingly, before it; and 'According to the Recipes of Ancient Greco-Syrian Magicians,' in which the poet Cavafy, neatly subsumed in the undiluted common denominator of an "aesthete," seeks the knowledge of past masters—can one doubt Shakespeare was one of these ancient magicians—in order to find his own way to realizing the end of the quest to which he has dedicated his life in art.

That this quest fully embraces as well as fundamentally emanates from Cavafy's sense of himself as a historical poet, or as Daniel Mendelsohn has recently suggested a poet-historian, can be easily observed by a reading of the complete list of the titles of his poems, and then substantially confirmed by a reading of the poems themselves. If poetry at its ground level quintessentially records our humanity, Cavafy's poetry gives us a history of our humanity through the singular perspectives his life afforded him. He belongs to that select group of poets who most directly draw us into living the lives of others, from the private, often obscure individual to the public luminary, from the anonymous to the eponymous. Memory, upon which stories of desire and the art of their telling depend, whom the craftsman apostrophizes in the name not only of his own effort but also of all of Cavafy's efforts before and after, is not, as the ancients saw it, the mother of his muses, but is herself his one and only muse.

Nourished by the long, interlaced narratives of Greek literature, culture, politics, and language, the historical poems clearly comprise the largest single group of poems Cavafy produced and manifestly represent the powerful inspiration of this muse, even when modified by the various familiar themes and approaches from his work as a whole that at times blend with them. But there is another significant dimension to her effect on him, which is to be found in how his writing reflects his special understanding of the poetry that has preceded him, those recipes of old, and his ability to write out of it, preferring to work with resonances of it rather than signatures of its influence. Nowhere does this fine modulation of his voice sound than in the numerous poems that show how carefully he read and subtly alluded to the amatory poets of ancient Greece, primarily those of the renowned *Greek*—also known as the *Palatine—Anthology*.

Ironically, Cavafy's only mentions of love poets from the *Greek Anthology* by name come in two poems that have nothing directly to do with love: Meleagros, in 'Symeon' as a better poet than the fictional Syrian Lamon, and again in 'Young Men of Sidon (400 A.D.)' along with Krinagoras and Rhianos, poets recognized for their eroticism, whose epigrams along with others constitute the program a professional actor has been hired to perform at a literary salon. Some critics have viewed this poem, especially its second half, in which one of the young men of Sidon passionately states his expectations of a literary artist, "Give—say I—all you have to your work,/ all your care, and keep your work in mind/ even during hardships, even as your time winds down./ This is what I expect and demand of you," as a passage of significant autobiographical import, notwithstanding the fact that the speech is actually an apostrophic address to the long departed Aeschylus, taking him to task for having composed his own epitaph exclusively as a tribute to his having fought in the Battle of Marathon. Though we are probably used to thinking of him as a complicated rather than a crafty Cavafy, perhaps in thinking about this poem we can conceive in it an intriguing invitation for us to imagine him, a child of the Greek diaspora himself, joining the company of the young men of Sidon in serious regard of their cultural heritage, having already apprenticed himself to the pastoral poet Theokritos, who appeared as a character in his poem 'The First Step' more than two decades before.

A different, equal at the least, order of interest arises when we respond to the invitation to consider the ways in which the poetry identified by the naming of a few of its makers actually affects Cavafy's writing, abandoning the admittedly often engrossing *explication de tête* in favor of *explication de texte*. To begin with, the compass of Cavafy's references to sexual attractions and actions matches that of the *Greek Anthology*, from lovers' rivalries and disagreements, for example, in 'Kimon, Son of Learchus, Age 22, Student of Greek Literature (in Cyrene)' and 'Lovely White Flowers So Well-Suited' to the recognition of time's destructive effect upon a beloved's or love object's beauty, usually but not always noted humorously with a vengeance by the poets in the anthology, a theme appropriated and stood on its head by Cavafy's counteracting exertions to preserve that beauty through memory and art. Between these come numerous poems that, it is important to stress, reflect not imitations but intimations of their parallels in the epigrams of the poets collected in the *Greek Anthology* and elsewhere: a passionate love that turns cool ('Before Time Could Change Them'), love celebrated for its uncompromising commitment or expertise and the power of Eros ('In the Dives—,' 'Days of 1901,' 'He Came to Read'), the importance of drinking, at times hard, during affairs and encounters ('I Went,' 'Half and Hour,' 'Two Young Men, 23 to 24 Years Old'), frustrated and unfulfilled love ('Desires,' 'On the Stairs,' 'The Afternoon Sun,'), love as fantasy and in dreams ('In the Theater,' 'Return,' 'When They Stir in Your Mind,' 'I've Gazed So Much,' 'Remember Body,' 'The Boring Village'), the use of *ekphrasis*, the description of visual and plastic arts, to highlight or enhance the aura and nature of love ('The Retinue of Dionysus,' 'Sculptor from Tyana,' 'At the Café Door,' 'Portrait of a Twenty-Three Year Old Painted by his Friend of the Same Age, An Amateur'), the eroticism of the gods ('One of their Gods'), and failed renunciations of love ('Dangerous Matters,' 'He Swears').

A short list of poets whose study could have activated this wide range of resonances might include Anakreon, Archilochos, Alkaios, Asclepiades, Dioskorides, Glaukos, Hedylos, Kallimachos, Meleagros, Philodemos, Poseidippos, Simonides, Straton, and the many anonymous poets whose epigrams were also collected in the anthology. But it is possible Cavafy's acquaintance with four of these poets may involve specific connections beyond the broad field of poetic interactions just considered. His characteristic antiheroic stance and theme may owe something to Archilochos and Kallimachos—to the former, the mercenary Iambic poet of Paros who wrote about how he blithely abandoned his shield under a bush during a battle with some wild Thracians, and to the latter, who, like Cavafy, moved to Alexandria as a young man and, unlike Cavafy, became a publicly renowned literary figure in his own time, and engaged in one of the great literary debates of antiquity, arguing for the superiority of the lyric over the epic. Demonstrative of Cavafy's dedication to this position ("I loathe the serial poem," Kallimachos begins one of his epigrams) is the fact that the longest poem he ever wrote is 91 lines long, the early 'King Claudius' (1899), which he wisely withheld from publication during his lifetime, leaving the honor of longest poem (70 lines) to 'Myres: Alexandria, 340 A.D.,' the magisterial dramatic monologue he wrote thirty years later. The third poet, Straton (fl. 125 A.D.), who compiled a famous anthology of homoerotic epigrams that eventually became part of the *Greek Anthology*, wrote a poem that offers a striking resemblance to Cavafy's finest poem that involves cruising and chance erotic encounters, 'He Asked About the Quality' (see also, 'On the Stairs,' 'In the Street,' 'The Tobacco Shop Window'). In my translation of Straton's poem, originally published in my Modern Library book of 2006, *Acts of Love*, which I quote below for the purposes of comparison, I changed the point of view from the first person to the third, retained here to complement the other similarities between the two poems.

> Earlier in the day, he happened to pass
> the store where they make garlands and saw a boy
> weaving flowers with berries, and found himself moved.
> He approached and asked about their quality,
> and then, somewhat more quietly, for how much
> would the boy sell him his garland. The boy blushed
> redder than his roses and, bending his head,
> told him to leave fast, lest his father see him.
> As a pretense he bought a wreath and went home,
> crowned his gods, and begged them to answer his prayer.

If this comes closer to source and analogue status than the other echoes of the old poets, there is also an unusually vivid similarity, separated by a profoundly different psychological sensibility, between the final lines of Cavafy's 'The Bandaged Shoulder,' a work he kept back with his other "unpublished" poems, and one of the anonymous epigrams in the anthology, in which the speaker crowns his beloved with ribbons after he's won a boxing match and gives "his bloodied-up face three kisses,/ but sweeter than myrrh it tasted to me."

Finally, the poem 'Gray' offers an important adversative illustration of Cavafy's response to his reading of the anthology poets. The resonance attunes us first to the principal image of an aging beloved's face, only the face in the sources is an unsightly, wrinkled one, usually described with cruel glee in revenge for the former beauty's haughty refusal to reciprocate the would-be lover's affection. These pungent lines by Archilochos, written during the middle of the seventh century B.C., "Gone's the bloom from your soft skin, your furrow's/ withered too, the … of foul old age is taking its toll,/] and the sweet loveliness has bolted from your longed for face," may well have set a model for later poets to follow, though some epigrams on this theme are tempered with ironic humor. But for Cavafy the image of the beloved and his once beautiful—doomed to be "broken down"—face has become instead an object to be preserved against time by memory.

> Gray
>
> Looking at a pale gray opal
> I remembered two beautiful gray eyes
> that I saw; must have been twenty years ago…
>
> ……………………………………………………
>
> We were lovers for a month.
> Then he took off, for Smyrna I think,
> for a job there, and we never saw each other again.
>
> They'll have lost their look—if he lives—those gray eyes;
> that beautiful face will have broken down.
>
> Memory, keep it the way it was.
> And, memory, whatever you can of that love,
> whatsoever you can, bring back to me tonight.

Invoking Memory, just as the craftsman does in the consummate expression of Eros, Memory, and Art, the nameless persona of this poem, like the speaker of 'Far Away,' who struggles to recall the eyes that were "deep dark blue, sapphire blue," stakes his case for remembrance on "those gray eyes" that he saw decades ago. While poems like 'Aboard Ship' and 'So They'll Come—' also depict the effort to recall and retain the image of the beloved, poems like 'Melancholy of Jason Cleander, Poet in Commagene, 595 A.D.,' in which an imaginary speaker in the distant past focuses on his own stressful, debilitating aging, a theme that resonates with numerous poems in the *Greek Anthology*, and hints somberly that the anodyne might be found in the art of poetry, and 'In Despair,' in which the persona hopelessly strives to regain a beloved who is lost to him altogether through liaisons with others, lay out what such seekers are up against in the starkest of terms, as in the refrain-like "never found again" in 'Days of 1903.' But in his apostrophe to Memory, the speaker in 'Gray' takes the first step towards restoration by his attempt to close the twenty-year separation of the lovers, denoted by the full line of periods, which also connotes the look on the page of many of the ancient lyrics by bringing to mind their irreparable lacunose state. If Art does not appear explicitly to play a role in this contest against time, as it does in 'Craftsman of Wine Bowls,' perhaps it is potentially there in 'Gray' nonetheless, virtually embodied by the poem itself.

A number of Cavafy's poems that involve imaginary poets and writers living in a fairly broad historical period beginning with the Hellenistic epoch and continuing well into the Christian era of the Byzantine Empire may also have been patterned on the poets from the age of Justinian in what is known as the Cycle of Agathias Scholastikos in the *Greek Anthology*. These poets, the best known of which was Paulos Silentiarius, were Christian and often held positions of importance, but also wrote erotic poems richly loaded with invocations of the pagan gods in the style and in emulation of the language of their predecessors, though, as W. R. Paton observes in the preface to his 1916 Loeb Classical Library edition of the anthology, they "wrote in a language which they did not command, but by which they were commanded, as all who try to write ancient Greek are." The challenges of writing in Greek for these fictional individuals and, in some cases, their contemporaries, are variously addressed in the poems 'He's the Man,' 'For Ammonis, Who Died at 29 in 610,' 'A Byzantine Noble, In Exile, Versifying,' while the young writer of 'Theatre of Sidon (400 A.D.)' boasts about his "extremely audacious verses" in the Greek language and the speaker and intimate friend of the poet in 'Temethus, Antiochian: 400 A.D.' haughtily explains Temethus' use of the pseudonym Emonides for his beloved, both without a hint of how demanding those tasks might have been.

Contrasting with the perspective in his historical poems that touch upon the diverse demands of speaking and writing in Greek and partaking of Greek culture in the Hellenized world, none of which is more poignant than the almost comical 'A Prince from Western Libya,' are numerous poems that indicate Cavafy's abiding interest in the writers of the literary movement during the first three centuries of our era known as the Second Sophistic, though when he first mentions them in his unpublished essay 'A Few Pages on the Sophists' (1893-97) he simply refers to them as the "later Sophists whose lives were passed down to us by Philostratus and Eunapius." In expressing his great sympathy for the generally despised sophists but particularly for the figures who now constitute the more fully recognized and better appreciated Second Sophistic, Cavafy was somewhat ahead of his time in his desire to counteract their bad luck and the poems he wrote that were influenced through his study of them confirm that he regarded their work "as a treasure trove of poetic material," as he specifically described *The Life of Apollonius* by Philostratus in his 1892 published essay on John Keats' poem 'Lamia.' Perhaps the observation he makes later in the same essay that "Poets fashion their own perceptions upon which they then build; they are entitled to delight in the reworking of material with full freedom," aptly defines his own artistic relationship with his sources, particularly those that comprise the cultural, historical, and literary legacy of his Greek identity.

While a number of poems like 'The God Abandons Antony,' 'He's the Man,' 'King Demetrius,' 'But Wise Men Apprehend What Is Imminent,' 'Apollonius of Tyana in Rhodes,' and 'Come, O King of the Lacedaimonians' connect with important figures in the Second Sophistic such as Lucian, Plutarch, and Philostratus through the use of direct quotations as titles, epigraphs or as part of the poetic text, and others like 'Demaratus' and 'Sophist Leaving Syria' explore activities of aspiring sophists, Cavafy affirms a special place of primacy for the most admired, renowned, prosperous, and influential individual of the Second Sophistic, Herodes Atticus, by devoting an entire poem to him.

Herodes Atticus

What a glorious rave is this for Herodes Atticus.

Alexander of Seleucia, one of our better sophists,
having gotten to Athens to lecture,
finds a deserted city, because Herodes
had gone to the country. And all the young men
had followed him there to hear him.
So then the sophist Alexander
writes Herodes a letter,
asking him to send back the Greeks.
Subtle Herodes answers directly,
"I'm coming, too, along with the Greeks."—

How many lads now in Alexandria,
in Antioch, or in Beirut
(tomorrow's Greek-trained orators),
when they gather at elite banquets
where the talk is sometimes about fine sophistry,
and sometimes about their exquisite love affairs,
distracted they suddenly fall silent.
They leave the glasses near them untouched,
and muse over Herodes' fortune—
what other sophist was so deserving?—
Whatever he wishes and whatever he does
the Greeks (the Greeks!) will follow him,
neither to criticize nor to discuss,
nor to choose any more, just to follow.

Surely the irony of his writing a poem completely devoted to a sophist famous for his role in building aqueducts, stadiums, and theaters but who is represented in the literary record by a single extant speech as opposed to the voluminous surviving works of the other sophistic authors he referred to and quoted was not lost on Cavafy. Taking a cue from an episode in *The Lives of the Sophists* of Philostratus, the twentieth-century Alexandrian poet gives the famous second-century Romanized Athenian luminary the rave review he deserves for his leading role in the *paideia* of Greeks who are not merely Greeks "in an ethnic sense" but "learning how to *become* Greeks in the full, cultural meaning of the word," as Tim Whitmarsh puts it in his book *The Second Sophistic*. It is in this sense that Alexander and Herodes used the word "Greeks" in their exchange of letters in the poem. If Cavafy's incorporation of writings by the sophists in his work offers us further insight into his involvement with his historical heritage, his distinctive emulation of one of their most important forms of public performance, declarations in fictitious or historical persona of narratives, many of whose themes dealt with the Persian War and the conquests of Philip of Macedon and Alexander the Great, meant to preserve the cultural identity of Greece, represents a deeper and more significant relationship with the phenomenon of the Second Sophistic. Cavafy, in effect, became one of them, but with a profound difference in point of view and purpose that the intervening centuries inevitably shaped. In carrying on their initiative, he did so by writing the many poems that explore the legacy of the past through pictures, large and small, of the lives of imaginary and historical characters that reveal its complexities and contradictions with pathos and irony.

The full extent of Cavafy's wide and deep appreciation of the Second Sophistic's devotion to culture and art, however, may also be perceived from point to point in the echo of a detail that he had once noted in Philostratus that the sophist Polemon rode in a chariot "with silver-mounted bridles," in the poem 'Facing the Statue of Endymion,' in which the fictitious speaker announces, "In a white chariot drawn by four/ milk-white, silver-harnessed mules/ I've arrived at Latmus from Miletus," all the way to the poet's praise for its commitment to the grandeurs of lifestyle and understanding of Art, an existential state expressed in perfect pitch by the second stanza of the poem: " I sailed in a purple trireme from Alexandria/ for sacred rites—sacrifices and libations—to Endymion./ Look, the statue. Thrilled, I now take in/ Endymion's renowned beauty./ My slaves empty baskets of jasmine; auspicious/ cheers awaken the pleasures of ancient times."

Although Cavafy's inspiration to build and rework numerous of his own poems such as 'The Retinue of Dionysus,' 'Sculptor from Tyana,' and 'Philhellene,' among others, some of which are set in later periods, further demonstrates the importance of this "advanced artistic disposition" for him, the esteem in which he held it provided him with a means of connecting it with his own time. For, as he continues in his commentary on the Sophists, they lived solely and passionately for the sake of Art and their worship of it "should endear them greatly to those of us who presently occupy ourselves with the Word." Spanning over approximately a thousand and a half years later to the days during which Cavafy began his artistic career, this correspondence not only helps define the purview from which he made poetry that contained and continued, in the language of the Greek diaspora, the diverse facets of the classical tradition as it was studied and interpreted in nineteenth-century Great Britain, but also admonishes us to pursue our intuitions and perceptions of the ways in which his singular complexity enabled him to freely build a poetic vision that stands apart and on its own. The influence of the Victorians and the Decadents, of writers like Robert Browning, John Addington Symonds, Arthur Symons, Oscar Wilde, Lord Alfred Douglas, Lionel Johnson and so many others has been and continues to be the subject of intense critical scholarship and has spoken and will speak better for itself, as do numerous studies of other aspects of Cavafy, than I can here. Yet it would be negligent not to consider Cavafy's link to the poet whose work profoundly influenced that of his own as well as the preceding and subsequent generations. Charles Baudelaire's *Fleurs du Mal* was not so shocking to him, Cavafy wrote in a 1907 unpublished note to himself, and indeed he found that compared to his own range of actual and imagined sensuality the French poet's was quite limited. If he was not exactly willing to be Baudelaire's *semblable,* he was indeed his *frère* in following in the footsteps of "the first true city poet " whose example "of the self as an antiheroic or problematic presence" (in the words of Jerome Rothenberg and Jeffrey C. Robinson in *Poems for the Millennium*, Vol. 3) he was to take as a foothold from which to write many of his poems. Though cities from the past like Antioch and Ptolemaic Alexandria provided him with settings for various poems, both historical, sensual and as composites of the two, his own Alexandria was the city the beauty of "whose masses, of poor young men" that so greatly pleased and moved him, as he avers in the personal note that immediately follows the one on Baudelaire. Though one can follow the course of the poems Cavafy wrote on this subject over the years, culminating with the great poem 'Days of 1908' that crowns them, a poem (dated May 1918) that might have most fittingly represented the city in the terms marked out by the effect on him by Baudelaire was one of those Cavafy began but never finished. The text that follows below has not been included with the translations of the poems in this book because I have chosen not to translate the elements of a never fully realized poem in Greek, especially when those elements consist of several unfinished and partially contradictory drafts, variants and marginalia. I have preferred, rather, to refashion those elements into a poem finished by me, an available hand educated for its execution, I hope, by my dedication during the last several years to the study and translation of Cavafy's poetry. While I do not claim my poem represents how Cavafy would have finished his preliminary workings of it, I will claim that my fully realized poem in English presents a text more true than traitorous to the poetic potency of its fragments.

The Newspaper Story

Dejected, reading the newspaper while riding the tram:
he came across an apparent crime in the Police Blotter,
a crime that had taken place the night before
between ten and eleven. The murderer had not yet been found.
The newspaper story, quite justly,
abhorred the murder, but righteously
showed its utter contempt
for the victim's degenerate way of life,
for that individual's depravity.

He read all about it, the contempt … and grieving in silence,
remembered an evening between ten and midnight a year ago
they had spent together in a room
(the only time—barely knowing each other by sight)
in a half-hotel, half brothel. Never—not even
in the street—did they ever meet again.
It described the wound in detail
and surmised blackmail must have had something to do with it.
The contempt … and he, grieving in silence,
remembered the sweet lips and the white, exceptional
sublime flesh he hadn't kissed enough.

Dejected, he read the story in the newspaper.
The body was discovered at about eleven at night
near the docks. It was not definite after all
that a crime had been committed,
a slight chance it was an accident, wasn't intentional.
The newspaper expressed some pity, but righteously
showed its indignation and contempt
for the victim's degenerate way of life.

The unidentified reader (and the barely distinguishable person who gives voice to his thoughts) in the poem, evidently in some way at odds with society and out of step with its mores, over the wall of whose shoulder we can perhaps read not only the immediate story in the newspaper but also those of a world of worlds, has he, with his passionate patience, created freely enough to entangle us in the wait for the advent of one who will create even more freely?

*

Secondary Sources

The source of the epigraph by George Steiner is his review 'Marrow versus marrow,' *TLS*, August 3, 2012, No 5705, p.9.

Cavafy, C. P., *Selected Prose Works*, translated and annotated by Peter Jeffreys (Ann Arbor: The University of Michigan Press, 2010). I have quoted from the following selections in this valuable work, 'Philosophical Scrutiny: Part One,' pp. 116-119; 'A Few Pages on the Sophists,' pp.112-115; 'Lamia,' pp. 43-53; and 'Twenty-Seven Notes on Poetics and Ethics,' pp.129-139).

Economou. George, 'Eros, Memory, and Art,' *The American Poetry Review* (July/August, 1981), Vol.10/ No. 4, 30-34.

Hirst, Anthony, 'Cavafy's Cavafy versus Savidis's Cavafy: The need to De-edit the "Acknowledged' Poems,"' *greekworks.com*, Arts & Letters, Friday, March 10, 2002.

_____, 'Philosophical, historical and sensual: an examination of Cavafy's thematic collections,' *Byzantine and Modern Greek Studies* 19 (1995), 33-93.

Rothenberg, Jerome and Jeffrey C. Robinson, *Poems for the Millennium*, Vol. 3 (Berkeley: University of California Press, 2009), Commentary on Charles Baudelaire, 607-608.

Whitmarsh, Tim. *The Second Sophistic*, New Surveys in the Classics No. 35 (Cambridge: Cambridge University Press, 2005).

*

The following list of editions of Cavafy's poetry was used for this book: George Savidis, *Poems*: Vol, I (1897-1918), Vol. II (1919-1933), 1991; *Hidden Poems*, (1877-1923), 1993; and *Rejected Poems*, 1983, all published in Athens under the Ikaros imprint. C. P. Cavafy, *The Collected Poems*, with a new translation by Evangelos Sachperoglou, Greek Text edited and with an introductory note (pp. xxxiv-xxxix) and Chronological List of Poems (pp. 23-234) by Anthony Hirst, (Oxford: Oxford University Press, 2007). *Ateli Poiemata* (*Unfinished Poems*), *1918-1932*, edited by Renata Lavagnini, (Athens: Ikaros Press. 1994).

*

The debt I owe to Vassilis Lambropoulos, C. P. Cavafy Professor of Modern Greek, and Artemis Leontis, both on the faculty of the University of Michigan, Ann Arbor, cannot be measured in words, though words can express it. For the last fifteen years, their advice, encouragement, and friendship have been staples of my life as a poet and translator. Their example as critics, scholars, and teachers has not only inspired me but has also tangibly affected whatever I have been able to accomplish. For this book, the latest of my impositions upon them for guidance and support, they have been unstinting in their willingness to assist a friend. Expert help has always been but an e-mail message or telephone call away. For their contribution to what has been our common cause in Greek and Greek American letters I can only thank and keep on thanking them.

I have been fortunate to know Stavros Deligiorgis ever since we met, *by aventure*, going on forty-five years ago at a conference in Kalamazoo, where both of us gave papers on Chaucer. We have kept our long friendship alive and lively through more ways than I can enumerate here, but will specify that a mutual love of poetry and the art and practice of translating it has been at the center of its gravity, one of the forces behind its longevity. Working together on this book of translations of poems by Cavafy did not happen by chance but is an outcome of this long and loyal friendship. Having benefited from his critical reading and advice when I was working on two previous small collections of translations from Cavafy, I asked him for his assistance once again. His generous and intense application of his superb command of all of the Greek language to this book, his keen detailed reading and re-reading of the versions of Cavafy's poems in it, not to mention his understanding of the very few times I decided, perhaps at my peril, not to take his advice, has proved so essential to my sense of its fulfillment that I made a proposal, to which he agreed, that his name be added to the cover and the title page. We both laughed heartily at his closing remark, "So they can have someone to blame?" The mark of his intelligence and learning inheres in many parts of this book, and once again I thank him, as I did twelve years ago, for teaching me the great Pythagorean lesson, ΚΟΙΝΑ ΤΑ ΤΩΝ ΦΙΛΩΝ.

—George Economou

for Rochelle

The Poems

Ode and Elegy of the Street

Footsteps of the first passer-by,
the first vendor's lusty cry,
the first opening of windows
and of doors—these are the songs
that morning streets sing.

The tread of the last passer-by,
the last vendor's last cry,
the closing of doors and windows,
these you hear are elegy's sounds
that belong to evening streets.

(1896)

Walls

Thoughtless, pitiless, indecent,
they put up high, thick walls around me.

And now I sit here and despair.
I think of nothing else: this condition just eats me up—

I had so many things to do outside.
How did I not pay attention when they were putting up the walls?

But of their building I never heard a noise or sound.
I hadn't a clue they were closing me off from the world outside.

(1897)

An Old Man

Some way inside the noisy coffeehouse
an old man sits bent over a table,
a newspaper before him, all alone.

And contemptuous of his desolate old age
he thinks about how little he enjoyed the years
when he was strong, articulate, and handsome.

He knows how much he's aged, feels it, sees it.
And yet the time he was young seems like
yesterday. How brief the span, how brief the span.

And he ponders how Forethought tricked him,
and how he always trusted it--what a fool---
that liar who said, "Tomorrow. You've lots of time."

He recalls impulses he held back, how much
joy he sacrificed. Every missed chance
now mocks his mindless good sense.

…But so much thinking and remembering
makes the old man woozy. And he falls asleep
leaning on the coffeehouse table.

(1897)

Achilles' Horses

       When they saw Patroclus killed,
who had been so valiant, and strong, and young,
    Achilles' horses began to weep,
        their deathless nature offended
by having to look upon this work of death.
    They tossed their heads and shook their long manes,
       they pounded the earth with their hooves, and mourned
Patroclus whom they saw lifeless—wiped out—
mere flesh now—his spirit lost—
        defenseless—without breath—
thrown back from life into the big Nothing.

    Zeus saw the tears of those immortal
horses and felt sad. "At Peleus' wedding,"
he said, "I shouldn't have acted so rashly;
    better for us not to have given you,
my unlucky horses! What were you doing down there
anyhow with that miserable human race, destiny's plaything.
      You for whom neither death nor old age lie in wait,
fleeting disasters torment now. Men have entangled
you in their ordeals."—Yet they kept shedding
    their tears for death's eternal
havoc, those two noble animals.

(1897)

Prayer

The sea took a sailor down to her depths.—
His mother, unaware, goes and lights

a tall candle before the Virgin Mother
for his quick return and for good weather—

and ever towards the wind she cocks her ear.
But while she pleads and says her prayer,

the icon listens, sad and solemn,
knows the son she awaits will never come.

(1898)

Sarpedon's Funeral

Heavy grief for Zeus. Patroclus
has killed Sarpedon; and now Menoetius'
son and the Achaians are rushing in
to carry off and degrade the body.

But to Zeus this is not at all acceptable.
His beloved child—that he allowed
to perish, such was the Law—
he will at least honor in death.
And look, he sends Phoebus down to the plain
with instructions for the body's tending.

Piously and sorrowfully Phoebus lifts
and carries the dead hero's body to the river.
He washes away the dust and blood;
he closes the terrible wounds, leaving
no trace in sight; he pours ambrosial
perfumes on him; and dresses him
in resplendent Olympian gowns.
He whitens his skin, and with a mother of pearl
comb combs his jet black hair.
He arranges and lays out his lovely limbs.

Now he resembles a young royal charioteer—
twenty-five or twenty-six years old—
at rest after winning,
with an all-gold chariot and the fastest horses,
the prize in a famous contest.

Having thus completed his task,
Phoebus invited the two brothers,
Sleep and Death, commanding them
to take the body to the rich land of Lycia.

And so towards that rich land, Lycia,
they marched, those two brothers
Sleep and Death, and when they arrived
at the door of the royal house
they turned over the glorious body,
and returned to their other cares and work.

And when it was received there, in the house,
there began, with processions, honors, and laments,
with profuse libations from sacred vessels,
and with the appropriate rites, the sad burial;
and then skilled city craftsmen
and renowned master stone-carvers came
and built the tomb and the stela.

(1898)

Candles

Our future days stand before us
like a row of lighted little candles—
golden, warm, bright little candles.

Past days remain behind,
a mournful line of blown out candles,
the nearest smoldering still,
cold candles, melted and bent over.

I don't want to look at them; the sight of them saddens me,
as does recalling their former light.
I look ahead at my still lighted candles.

I don't want to turn to see, and shudder
at how quickly the dark line grows longer,
at how quickly the blown out candles wax.

(1899)

The First Step

One day the young poet Eumenes
was complaining to Theokritos:
"For the past two years I've been writing
and have produced a single idyll.
It's my only finished work.
Alas, I see how very high it reaches,
poetry's ladder, so very high.
Pathetic, I'll never rise above
this first step I'm standing on now."
Theokritos replied: "Such language
is unbecoming, blasphemous.
So what if you're on the first step,
that should make you proud and happy.
No small thing to have got this far,
what you have achieved is indeed glorious.
And even this very first step
stands far above the common crowd.
Just to ascend to this step,
you must be a rightful citizen
of the city of ideas.
And difficult and rare it is
to become one of its citizens.
In its chambers are legislators
that no opportunist can fool.
No small thing to have got this far,
what you have achieved is glorious indeed."

(1899)

The Souls of Old Men

Inside their old threadbare bodies
sit the souls of old men.
How distressed the poor things are
and how fed up with the wretched life they lead.
How they tremble to lose it and how they love it
those bewildered and conflicted
souls that sit—tragicomically—
inside their old, ravaged hides.

(1901)

Che Fece ... Il Gran Rifuto

For some people there comes a day
when they must say the great Yes
or the great No. It's immediately apparent
who has the Yes ready within and in saying it

attains his honor and his conviction.
He who refuses does not repent. Asked again,
he'd say no again. Even though that no—
the right no—lays him low all his life.

(1901)

Interruption

We interrupt the work of the gods,
we hasty, callow beings of the moment.
In the palaces of Eleusis and Phthia
Demeter and Thetis begin good works
amid high flames and thick smoke. But then
Metaneira always dashes in from the royal
rooms, hair unkempt and terrified,
and Peleus always gets scared and butts in.

(1901)

The Windows

In this dark flat of mine, I pass
gloomy days going in circles
looking for the windows.—If only one
were to open it would be some relief.—
But the windows can't be found, or I just can't
find them. Maybe it's best I don't find them.
The light could turn out to be some new oppression.
Who knows what new things that might show.

(1903)

Thermopylae

Honor to those who in their lives
decide on and defend Thermopylae.
Never recoiling from their duty,
just and steadfast in all their deeds,
but with pity and compassion as well;
generous when they're rich, and when
they're poor, generous still in small ways,
helping again as best they can;
always speaking the truth,
but without hatred for liars.

And they deserve greater honor
when they foresee (and many do foresee)
that Ephialtes will show up in the end,
and the Medes will eventually break through.

(1903)

Perfidy

Then, though there are many other things we praise in Homer, this we will not applaud... nor shall we approve of Aeschylus when his Thetis avers that Apollo, singing at her wedding, foretold the happy fortunes of her issue,

"Their days prolonged, from pain and sickness free,
And rounding out the tale of heaven's blessings.
Raised the proud paean, making glad my heart.
And I believed that Phoebus' mouth divine,
Filled with the breath of prophecy, could not lie.
But he himself, the singer...
Is now... the slayer of my son."

    Plato, *Republic*, II, 383b
    (translation by Paul Shorey)

When they were marrying Thetis and Peleus
Apollo rose at the glorious bridal
banquet and called the pair of newlyweds blessed
for the scion their union would produce.
He said, "No disease will ever touch him
and he will have a long life." This being said,
Thetis was overjoyed because the words
of Apollo, who knows all about prophecies,
seemed to her a surety for her child.
And when Achilles had grown up,
and his good looks were the praise of Thessaly,
Thetis remembered the god's very words.
But one day some old men arrived with news
about the killing of Achilles at Troy.
And Thetis ripped apart her purple clothes,
and tore off all of her rings and bracelets,
and dashed them to the ground.
And in her grief remembered old days,
and asked what was Apollo the wise doing,
where was he wandering, the poet who
spoke so well at feasts, where was the prophet off to

when they killed her son in his youthful prime.
And the old men answered her that Apollo
himself had descended to Troy
and with the Trojans had killed Achilles.

(1904)

Waiting for the Barbarians

—What are we waiting for, assembled in the Forum?

    The barbarians are supposed to come today.

—Why is the Senate so idle?
    Why do the Senators just sit there passing no laws?

    Because the barbarians arrive today.
    Why should the Senators make laws anymore?
    Once they get here, the barbarians will make the laws.

—Why did our Emperor arise so early
    and sit ceremoniously on the throne
    at the city's main gate wearing his crown?

    Because the barbarians arrive today.
    And the Emperor waits to receive
    their leader. Indeed, he's prepared
    a scroll to give him. On it
    he's ascribed to him numerous names and titles.

—Why have our two consuls and praetors come out
    today in their scarlet, embroidered togas?
    Why do they wear bracelets with so many amethysts
    and rings with splendid glittering emeralds?
    Why should they hold priceless scepters today,
    superbly engraved in silver and gold?

    Because the barbarians arrive today,
    and such things dazzle the barbarians.

—Why haven't our worthy orators shown up as always
    to turn out their speeches, to have their usual say?

Because the barbarians arrive today
   and eloquence and public speaking bore them.

—Why so suddenly this anxiety
   and this confusion? (How serious faces have become.)
   Why do the streets and squares empty so fast,
   and why has everyone returned home so preoccupied?

   Because it's nightfall and the barbarians haven't come.
   And some people have arrived from the frontier
   and said that barbarians no longer exist.

   So now what happens to us without barbarians?
   Those people were a kind of solution.

(1904)

Voices

Voices beloved and of a perfect kind
of those who have died, or of those
who are as lost to us as are the dead.

At times they speak to us in a dream;
at times, in thought, the mind hears them.

And with their sound, for a second, sounds
return from the first poetry of our life—
like faraway music that fades in the night.

(1904)

Desires

Like beautiful bodies of the dead who didn't age
and were tearfully enclosed in a splendid mausoleum,
with roses at the head, jasmine at the feet—
so seem our desires that have passed
without fulfillment, without a single one granted
the pleasure of a night, or of a sunny morning.

(1904)

On the Stairs

As I descended those shameful stairs,
you were coming through the door, and for a second
I saw your unfamiliar face, and you saw me.
Then I hid from your seeing me again, and you
passed by quickly, hiding your face,
and slipped into that shameful house
where you would find no pleasure, just as I had not.

Yet the love you sought was mine to give you;
the love I sought—betrayed by your eyes,
so weary and worldly—was yours to give me.
Our bodies sensed and yearned for each other,
our blood and skin knew it.

But, flustered, we both hid ourselves.

(1904)

In the Theater

I got tired of looking at the stage,
and raised my eyes up to the boxes.
And in one of them I saw you
with your strange beauty, your ravaged youth.
And right away I recalled
what was said about you that afternoon,
and I was stirred, body and soul.
And as I gazed under the spell
of your weary beauty, your worn out youth,
your stylish way of dressing,
I imagined and pictured you
in the ways they talked about you that afternoon.

(1904)

Trojans

Our efforts are those of men headed for disaster;
our efforts are like those of the Trojans.
We succeed a little, pick up
a little strength and start
to feel daring and rather hopeful.

But something always comes up and stops us.
Achilles jumps out of the moat in front of us
and frightens us with his enormous shouts.—

Our efforts are like those of the Trojans.
We think that with resolve and bravery
we'll change our malignant luck
and we move out to take up the fight.

But when the great crisis happens,
our bravery and resolve disappear;
our spirit gets worried, paralyzed,
and we run around the walls
trying to save ourselves through flight.

But our fall is certain. Up above,
on the walls, the dirge has already begun.
The memories and feelings of our days wail.
Bitterly for us Priam and Hecuba wail.

(1905)

King Demetrius

> *As if he were not a king but an actor who put on a grey cloak
> instead of the robe of tragedy, slipped away unnoticed.*
> Plutarch, *Life of Demetrius*, XLIV

When the Macedonians deserted him
and showed they preferred Pyrrhus,
King Demetrius (great soul
that he was) did not at all—so they said—
behave like a king. He went
and took off his golden robes
and threw away his boots
of deep purple. He quickly put on
simple clothes and gave them the slip.
Doing just as an actor does
when the show is over,
he changes outfits and leaves.

(1906)

The Retinue of Dionysus

Damon the artisan (there's none better
in the Peloponnese) is putting the final
touches on his Retinue of Dionysus
in Parian marble. The god, divinely glorious
in the lead, with strength in his gait.
Unmixed Wine right behind. Beside him
Intoxication pours the Satyrs wine
from an amphora wreathed in ivy.
Near them is Sweetwine, the effete,
his eyes half-shut, somnolent.
And down the line come the singers
Crooner and Melody and Reveller
who never lets the revered processional torch
he holds go out, then Solemnity, most modest.—
These Damon works on. And as he does
his thoughts every now and then fasten
on his compensation from the King
of Syracuse, three talents, a big sum.
When deposited with the rest of his money,
he'll live the rich man's life in style,
and he'll go into politics—wow!—
and be in the Senate, and in the public market-place.

(1907)

Monotony

One monotonous day follows after another
with identical monotony. The same
things will happen and happen again—
the same moments will come to us and go.

A month goes by and it brings another month.
It's easy to guess what lies ahead:
the stuff of yesterday's tedium. And tomorrow
ends up looking nothing like tomorrow.

(1908)

Hidden Things

From what I said and from what I did
let them not try to find who I was.
A barrier went up and altered
my actions and my way of life.
A barrier went up and prevented
me so many times from speaking my mind.
The least noticed of my actions,
and the most veiled of my writings—
from these alone they'll feel as I have felt.
But maybe it wouldn't be worth taking
so much trouble and effort to know me.
Later—in a more perfect world—
anybody else made just like me
will surely appear and will create freely.

(1908)

The Footsteps

On an ebony bed embellished
with coral eagles, in a deep sleep
lies Nero—unscrupulous, at peace, and happy,
his strength of body at its peak,
and in the lovely vigor of youth.

But in the alabaster hall that holds
the ancient shrine of the Aenobarbi
how uneasy are his Lares.
The little household gods tremble,
and try to hide their minuscule bodies.
Because they heard a horrible noise,
a deadly noise coming up the stairs,
iron footsteps that jolt the staircase.
And now, faint with fear, the forlorn Lares
push their way into the back of the shrine,
jostling and bumping into one another,
one little god falls upon another.
Because they understand what kind of noise that is.
They know by now the footsteps of the Furies.

(1909)

He's the Man

Unknown—a stranger in Antioch—this Edessene
writes, writes, writes. Finally, there it is, the last
canto is finished. With that eighty-three

poems in all. But the poet's all worn out
by so much writing, so much versifying,
such strain from turning phrases into Greek,
and now every last thing's just a burden.—

Yet a single thought suddenly lifts him
out of his doldrums—that superb "He's the Man,"
which Lucian once heard in his sleep.

(1909)

The City

You said, "I'll go to another land, I'll go to another sea.
Another city will turn up, better than this.
Everything I do is doomed to fail,
and my heart—like a dead man—lies in a grave.
How long can my mind go on stagnating here?
Wherever I look, wherever my eye falls,
all I see is this black wreck of a life,
here where I've spent these years, wasted them, ruined them."

You'll not find other places, you won't find other seas.
This city will shadow you. You'll walk the same
old streets. In the same old neighborhoods you'll age,
in the same old houses you'll turn gray.
You'll always end up in this city. As for elsewhere—no hope—
there's no ship for you, nor road to take.
Thus, as you've wasted your life
in this tiny corner, you've ruined it throughout the face of the earth.

(1910)

The Satrapy

What a bad outcome, that though you were born
to do beautiful and great things
this unfair fate of yours always
denies you encouragement and success;
that nasty customs hamper you,
and meanness, and indifference.
And how terrible the day you give in
(the day you give up and give in)
and hit the road for Susa,
to go to King Artaxerxes
who happily installs you in his court,
and offers you satrapies and such.
And you despairingly accept
what you have no desire for.
Your soul seeks and cries out for other things:
the praise of the Demos and the Sophists,
that hard-won and priceless "Hear! Hear!"
the Agora, the Theatre, the Garlands.
How will Artaxerxes give you these,
how will you find them in a satrapy,
what kind of life will you have without them?

(1910)

The Ides of March

Of things grandiose be afraid, my soul.
And if you can't master your ambitions,
pursue them with hesitation and precaution.
And the further you get ahead,
be that much more questioning and careful.

And when you have peaked, a Caesar at last,
and have assumed the figure of a famous man,
then be careful above all as you step out into the street,
a noteworthy ruler with a retinue,
if by chance a certain Artemidorus
approaches out of the crowd bearing a letter,
and says very fast, "Read this right away,
important things concerning you,"
don't fail to pause; don't fail to postpone
all talk or business; don't fail to brush off
the various greeters and grovellers
(you can see them later); let even the Senate
itself wait, and find out at once
what's in Artemidorus' serious message.

(1911)

Finished

In the midst of fear and misgivings,
with mind in turmoil and terrified eyes,
we break down coming up with ways
to avoid the certain danger
menacing us so terribly.
Yet we're mistaken, that's not what lies ahead:
the news was untrustworthy
(or we didn't hear it, or didn't get it right).
Another catastrophe, which we never imagined,
unexpected, violently befalls us,
and unprepared—out of time now—blows us away.

(1911)

Sculptor from Tyana

You have heard, perhaps, a novice I'm not.
Plenty of stone has passed through my hands.
In my homeland of Tyana I'm quite
well-known, and local Senators
have commissioned many statues.
Let me show you
a few right now. Have a look at this Rhea:
venerable, full of forbearance, primordial.
Take note of Pompey. Of Marius,
of Aemilius Paulus, of Scipio Africanus.
True likenesses, to the best of my ability.
And Patroclus (I'll touch him up a bit).
Near those pieces of yellowish marble
over there, is Caesarion.

And for some time now I've been engaged
with creating a Poseidon. I'm studying
his horses especially, how to contrive them.
They have to be done so light
that their bodies, their feet clearly show
they're not treading ground but running on water.
But now here's my most beloved work
that I have crafted with emotion and greatest care.
Him, one hot summer day,
as my mind was soaring to the ideal,
him here I was dreaming of, young Hermes.

(1911)

The God Abandons Antony

Should you suddenly at midnight hear
an unseen procession passing
with exquisite music, with cries—
about your luck that's running out, about your work
that's gone awry, about your lifetime plans
that came to nothing, there's no point in complaining.
Like one long ready, one full of courage,
bid her farewell, this Alexandria that is leaving.
Above all, don't deceive yourself, don't say
it was an illusion, something you thought you heard:
don't demean yourself with such idle hopes.
Like one long ready, one full of courage,
as befits you, a man worthy of such a city,
stand firmly by the window
and listen with feeling, but not
pleading and whining like a coward,
as a final pleasure, to the strains
and exquisite instruments of that mystic procession.
Bid her farewell, this Alexandria you are losing.

(1911)

Ionic

So what if we've smashed their statues,
so what if we've thrown them out of their temples,
the gods are not dead on account of that..
Ionia, Ionia, they love you still,
in their souls they remember you still.
When an August morning breaks light on you,
the power of their lives fills your air,
and at times a young unearthly form,
hazy and fleeting,
glides above your hills.

(1911)

The Glory of the Ptolemies

I am the Lagid, king. Absolute lord
(with my power and wealth) of all pleasure.
No Macedonian or barbarian equals me,
or even comes close. And he's a joke,
the Seleucid with his street-bought joys.
But if it's more you want, take a look at what's clear.
The city's the teacher, of all things Greek the best,
of every study and every art the wisest.

(1911)

Ithaca

As you begin the journey to Ithaca,
pray for a road that will be long,
full of adventures, full of lessons.
Of Laistrygonians, of Cyclopes,
and livid Poseidon have no fear,
you'll never encounter such things on your course,
provided your thoughts remain high, and a rare
kind of excitement touches your body and mind.
Laistrygonians and Cyclopes,
savage Poseidon you'll not meet up with,
unless you carry them in your soul,
unless your soul raises them before you.

Pray for a road that will be long.
Let there be many summer mornings
when with such pleasure and such joy
you'll enter harbors seen for the very first time;
may you stop at Phoenician marketplaces,
and make fine bargains for goods,
mother-of-pearl and coral, amber and ebony,
and sensual perfumes of every kind,
as many sensual perfumes as possible;
may you go to many Egyptian cities,
to learn and learn from their great scholars.

Always keep Ithaca in your mind.
Getting there is your destination.
But by no means rush the journey.
Better to let it go on for years;
and as an old man to drop anchor at the island,
rich with all you've won along the way,
without expecting Ithaca to give you wealth.
Ithaca gave you the beautiful journey.
Without her you wouldn't have taken the road.
She has nothing more to give you.

And if you find her poor, she didn't deceive you.
Now that you have become so wise, so full of experience,
you'll understand what all these Ithacas mean.

(1911)

Dangerous Matters

Said Myrtias (a Syrian student
in Alexandria during the reigns
of the emperors Constans and Constantius;
partly pagan and partly Christianized):
"Strengthened by meditation and study,
I will not fear my passions like a coward.
I will give over my body to pleasures,
to the delights of which I dream,
to the most daring of erotic desires,
to the lustful urgings of my blood, without
a single fear, because when I want—
and I'll have the will, strengthened
as I'll be by meditation and study—
in moments of crisis I will regain
my spirit as it was before, ascetic."

(1911)

Philhellene

See to it the engraving's artfully done.
The expression solemn and grand.
Prefer the diadem somewhat narrow;
I don't like those in the broad Parthian style.
The inscription, as usual, in Greek:
nothing ostentatious, nothing pompous—
we don't want the proconsul to misconstrue it,
who's always poking around and informing Rome—
nevertheless, giving me due respect.
Something specially nice for the reverse:
say a handsome teenage discus-thrower.
Above all I urge you to make sure
(my god, Sithaspes, don't let them forget)
that after the words "King" and "Savior,"
"Philhellene" be engraved in elegant letters.
Now please don't start with your wisecracks,
your "Where are the Greeks?" and "Anything Greek
here behind the Zagros, beyond Phraata?"
If countless others, more barbarian
than we, can write it, then we'll write it too.
And in the end, don't forget that sometimes
sophists come to us out of Syria,
and versifiers, and other would-be intellectuals.
So we're not exactly un-Hellenized, it seems to me.

(1912)

Herodes Atticus

What a glorious rave is this for Herodes Atticus.

Alexander of Seleucia, one of our better sophists,
having gotten to Athens to lecture,
finds a deserted city, because Herodes
had gone to the country. And all the young men
had followed him there to hear him.
So then the sophist Alexander
writes Herodes a letter,
asking him to send back the Greeks.
Subtle Herodes answers directly,
"I'm coming, too, along with the Greeks."—

How many lads now in Alexandria,
in Antioch, or in Beirut
(tomorrow's Greek-trained orators),
when they gather at elite banquets
where the talk is sometimes about fine sophistry,
and sometimes about their exquisite love affairs,
distracted they suddenly fall silent.
They leave the glasses near them untouched,
and muse over Herodes' fortune—
what other sophist was so deserving?—
Whatever he wishes and whatever he does
the Greeks (the Greeks!) will follow him,
neither to criticize nor to discuss,
nor to choose any more, just to follow.

(1912)

Alexandrian Kings

The Alexandrians came together
to see Cleopatra's children,
Caesarion and his little brothers,
Alexander and Ptolemy, for the first
time brought out to the Gymnasium,
in order to proclaim them as kings there,
before a splendid military formation.

Alexander—him they declared the king
of Armenia, Media, and the Parthians.
Ptolemy—him they declared king
of Cilicia, Syria, and Phoenicia.
Caesarion stood well in front,
dressed in rose-colored silk,
a bouquet of hyacinths on his chest,
his belt a double row of sapphires and amethysts,
his shoes tied with white
ribbons embroidered with pink pearls.
Him they declared greater than the little ones,
him they declared King of Kings.

Of course the Alexandrians knew
all of this was just words and theatrics.

But the day was warm and poetic,
the sky a clear blue,
the Alexandrian Gymnasium
a triumphant artistic achievement,
the courtiers magnificently luxurious,
Caesarion all grace and beauty
(Cleopatra's son, blood of the Lagids);
and the Alexandrians rushed in to the festival,
full of enthusiasm, and cheered
in Greek, and Egyptian, and some in Hebrew,
captivated by the lovely spectacle—

knowing all the time of course the value of these things,
what empty words these kingdoms were.

(1912)

Return

Return often and take me,
beloved feeling return and take me—
when the body's memory awakes,
and old desire runs through the blood again,
when lips and skin remember,
and hands feel as if they touch once more.

Return often and take me at night,
when lips and skin remember....

(1912)

In Church

I love the church—her gilt six-winged banners,
her silver vessels, her candelabra,
her lights, her icons, and pulpit.

Whenever I go inside a Greek church:
what with the fragrances of incense,
the liturgical chanting and harmonies,
the grandeur of the priests' presence
and the solemn rhythm of their every movement—
resplendent in their ornate vestments—
my mind lays hold of the great honors of our race,
of the glory of our being Byzantine.

(1912)

Very seldom

He's an old man. Run down and bent.
Crippled by age and overindulgence,
he walks slowly down the narrow street.
But when he enters his house to hide
his misery and old age, he thinks about
the share in youth he still retains.

Young men quote his verse now.
His visions pass into their lively eyes.
His expression of beauty stirs
their healthy sensual minds,
their well-built shapely bodies.

(1913)

As Much As You Can

And if you can't manage your life the way you want,
at least try this as much
as you can: do not debase it
with too much give and take with the world,
with too much running around and talk.

Do not debase your life by yanking it
around and exposing it often
to the daily nonsense
of making connections and scenes,
until it becomes like a tiresome stranger.

(1913)

For the Shop

He wrapped them carefully, smartly
in green silk that was quite pricey.

Roses of rubies, lilies of pearl,
violets of amethyst. According to his rule,

his will, they seemed beautiful, still
not as in nature or books. In the till

he'll leave them, samples of his bold and able work.
Whenever some customer enters the shop

he brings out other fine items for sale—rich things—
bracelets, chains, necklaces and rings.

(1913)

I Went

I didn't hold back. I just let myself go and went.
To thrills that were half real,
half spun inside my own mind,
I went into the lit up night.
And drank strong wines, the way
pleasure's best and bravest drink.

(1913)

Tomb of Lysias the Grammarian

Coming up here on the right as you enter
Beirut Library, we buried learned Lysias,
the grammarian. A perfectly suitable site.
We put him near things of his he remembers
perhaps even there—notes, texts, books of grammatical analyses,
scripts, multi-volume studies of hellenisms.
And so this way, too, we'll see and pay our respects
to his tomb as we proceed to the books.

(1914)

Tomb of Eurion

In this most artfully made memorial,
entirely of syenite stone,
covered with so many violets and lilies,
is buried the handsome Eurion.
An Alexandrian youth of twenty-five.
On his father's side, from old stock Macedonian,
on his mother's, from a line of Jewish magistrates.
A student of Aristokleitus in philosophy,
of Parus in rhetoric. At Thebes he studied
the sacred scriptures. He wrote a history
of the Arsinoïte prefecture. At least that will last.
But we've lost what's most priceless—the figure he cut,
that was so like an Apollonian vision.

(1914)

Chandelier

In a small, empty room, just four walls,
draped in deep green cloths,
a beautiful chandelier burns and glows;
and in every one of its flames kindles
a lustful fervor, a lustful urge.

In the small room, lambent
with the chandelier's powerful fire,
this is no ordinary light that flows.
It wasn't made for timid bodies,
this heat's passionate pleasure.

(1914)

Far Away

Here's a memory I'd like to tell...
But it's so faint now... a mere nothing's left—
because it lies far away, in my early adolescence.

Skin as if made of jasmine...
That August evening—was it August?
I can barely remember the eyes: they were, I think, dark blue...
Ah yes, deep, dark blue: sapphire blue.

(1914)

Returning Home from Greece

Well, we're just about there, Hermippos.
Day after tomorrow, I expect. Like the captain said.
At least we're sailing in our own sea,
the waters of Cyprus, Syria, and Egypt,
beloved waters of our homelands.
Why so quiet? In your heart of hearts,
as we were moving away from Greece
weren't you happy, too? But why kid ourselves?—
 that just wouldn't be appropriately Greek.

So it's high time we admitted the truth:
we too are Greek—what else are we?—
but with affections and emotions out of Asia,
with affections and emotions
occasionally striking the Greeks of Greece as strange.

It's not fitting for us, Hermippos, for philosophers like us
to look like some of our petty despots
(remember how we laughed at them
when they'd drop by our academies)
behind whose appearance,

flashily Hellenized and (I should talk!) Macedonian,
a little bit of Arabia shows through now and then,
a little bit of Media cannot be held in check,
and with what comical ploys the poor things
try to keep it from being noticed.

Ah, no, such fakery is not fitting for us.
Such pettiness is not worthy of Greeks like us.
Of the Syrian and Egyptian blood
that runs through our veins, let's not be ashamed,
let's honor it and glory in it.

(1914)

But Wise Men Apprehend What Is Imminent

> *The gods perceive what lies in the future, and mortals, what occurs in the present, but wise men apprehend what is imminent.*
> —Philostratus, *The Life of Apollonius of Tyana*, VIII. 7

Humans know about the present.
The gods about the future,
full and sole keepers of all that's known.
About future things wise men apprehend
what's imminent. Their hearing

now and then in times of serious meditation
becomes excited. The secret hum
of things about to happen comes to them.
And they listen reverently. While in the street
outside, the people hear nothing.

(1915)

Theodotus

If you are one of the truly elect,
watch how you attain your preeminence.
However much you're glorified, however much
the cities acclaim your achievements
in Italy and Thessaly,
however many honorary decrees
your admirers in Rome turn out for you,
neither your joy nor your triumph will last,
nor will you feel like a superior— superior how?—person,
when, in Alexandria, Theodotus brings you
on a blood-stained charger
wretched Pompey's head.

And don't rest assured that in your
circumscribed, well-managed, and prosaic life
such spectacular and terrifying things don't happen.
Perhaps at this very moment into some
neighbor's spick-and-span house there comes—
invisible, immaterial—Theodotus,
carrying a similar grisly head.

(1915)

At the Café Door

Something they said beside me
turned my attention to the café door.
And I saw that lovely body that looked
as if Eros had made it at the height of his powers—
joyfully molding its elegant limbs,
sculpting its stature tall,
excitedly molding its face
and leaving by the touch of his hands
a certain feeling in the brow, the eyes, the lips.

(1915)

He Swears

Every so often he swears   he'll reform his life.
But when night comes   with its own counsels,
with its own compromises   and promises;
but when night comes   with its own force
of a body that desires and demands, to that same
fateful joy, lost, he returns.

(1915)

One Night

The room was seedy and sordid,
hidden above the suspect taverna.
From the window you could see the alley,
filthy and narrow. From below
came the voices of workmen
who were playing cards and partying.

And there on that ordinary, humble bed,
I had love's body, I had the lips,
so sensual, so red, intoxicating—
the red lips of such intoxication, that even now
as I write, after so many years!
in my lonely house, I am drunk again.

(1915)

Morning Sea

Might as well stand here. Take a little look myself at nature, too.
The morning sea and the cloud-free sky
a brilliant blue, and the shore yellow, all of it
lovely and grandly lighted.

Might as well stand here and fool myself I see all this
(I really did see it for a minute when I first stopped)
and not my fantasies right here, too,
my memories, those visions of sensuality.

(1915)

Painted

I'm careful about my art and love it.
But today I'm discouraged by how slowly it's materializing.
The day's affected me. It's looking
dark and darker. All wind and rain.
I feel a lot more like looking than talking.
In this painting I'm looking at now
a beautiful boy is lying down beside
a spring, after running till he dropped.
What a beautiful boy; what a sublime afternoon
has taken him at last to put him to sleep.—
I sit and look like this for a long time.
Once again, in art, I'm refreshed by my working at it.

(1915)

Orophernes

He who on this four drachma piece
seems to have a smile on his face,
his handsome, refined face,
he is Orophernes, son of Ariarathes.

A child, they ran him out of Cappadocia,
out of the great ancestral palace,
and sent him to grow up in Ionia,
to be forgotten among foreigners.

Ah, those splendid Ionian nights
when fearlessly, and in ways completely Greek
he experienced sensuality to the full.
In his heart, always Asiatic,
yet in his manners and speech, a Greek,
decked out in turquoise, dressed in Greek fashion,
his body fragrant with jasmine oil,
of all of Ionia's handsome young men,
he was the handsomest, the most perfect.

Later, when the Syrians entered
Cappadocia and made him king,
he threw himself into kingship
in order to enjoy himself anew each day,
in order to ravenously amass gold and silver,
and to gladden his heart and brag,
looking over glittering heaps of wealth.
As for looking after and managing the country—
he had no idea what was happening around him.

The Cappadocians promptly got rid of him;
and he wound up in Syria, at the palace
of Demetrius to hang out and amuse himself.

One day, however, unaccustomed thoughts
cut through his out and out idleness:
he recalled how through his mother Antiochis,
and through that ancient one Stratonice,
he also descended from the Syrian crown,
and was a Seleucid almost.
He briefly withdrew from lechery and drink,
and ineptly, half in a fog
he went for some sort of machination,
to do something, to contrive something,
and failed miserably, and was wiped out.

His end must have been recorded somewhere then lost;
or maybe history just passed it by,
and, quite rightly, refused to stoop
to take note of such a trivial matter.

He who on the four drachma piece
left something of his lovely youthful charm,
a flash of his poetic beauty,
a sensuous remembrance of an Ionian boy,
he is Orophernes, son of Ariarathes.

(1915)

The Battle of Magnesia

He's lost his spirit, his courage.
His tired old body on the verge

of sickness, his main concern now. The rest
of his life he'll spend without a care. At least

that's what Philip claims. Tonight he'll roll the dice;
he feels like having some fun. Throw lots of nice

roses onto the table. So what if at Magnesia
Antiochus was wasted. They say the carnage

most of his glorious army sustained was brutal.
Maybe that's overstated; not all of it truthful.

Let's hope so. They're still of our race, though an enemy.
But one "Let's hope so" suffices. Maybe one too many.

Philip, of course, won't put off the celebration.
No matter how much he's endured life's enervation,

one good thing remains, his memory's still sound.
He recalls their kind of sorrow in Syria, how they mourned

when their mother Macedonia was reduced to mites.—
Let the party begin. Slaves, the flutes, the lights.

(1915)

Manuel Comnenus

The king Lord Manuel Comnenus
one unhappy September day
sensed death nearby. The court astrologers
(on the payroll) kept on jabbering
about how many years he still had to live.
But while they were talking,
past revered customs come to mind,
and he orders churchly garments
be brought from the monastery cells,
and he wears them, deeply pleased he evinces
the modest bearing of a priest or monk.

Happy are all who believe,
and like the king Lord Manuel Comnenus
end their days dressed modestly in their faith.

(1915)

The Displeasure of the Seleucid

Demetrius the Seleucid was displeased
to learn that a Ptolemy had arrived
in Italy in such a pathetic state:
with only three or four slaves,
poorly dressed and on foot. This way
they'll end up as a joke, and their lineage
Rome's laughing-stock. That at bottom they've become
something like servants to the Romans
the Seleucid knows, that they're the ones
who give and take away their thrones
arbitrarily, just as they please, this he knows.
But at least let them keep up appearances
of a certain kind of majesty;
let them not forget that they are still kings,
that they are (alas!) still called kings.

That's what annoyed Demetrius the Seleucid;
and why he right away offered Ptolemy
purple robes, a glittering diadem,
costly jewelry, numerous
attendants and escorts, his most prized horses,
so he might show up in Rome appropriately,
as an Alexandrian Greek monarch.

But Ptolemy the Lagid, who came seeking handouts,
knew his business and refused everything:
he had no need at all for such luxuries.
Dressed in rags, humble, he entered Rome,
and lodged in a second-rate artisan's home.
He then presented himself to the Senate
as a pitiful, destitute person,
much the better to beg.

(1915)

When They Stir in Your Mind

Try to watch over them, poet,
however few there are that can be stayed.
The visions of your erotic life.
Slip them, half-hidden, into your phrases.
Try to hold on to them, poet,
when they stir in your mind
at night or in the noonday glare.

(1916)

In the Street

His attractive face, a little wan;
his chestnut eyes, sort of listless;
twenty-five, but could pass for twenty;
something artsy about his outfit
—that touch of color in his tie, his collar style—
he drifts aimlessly in the street,
as if still hypnotized by the illicit pleasure,
by the very illicit pleasure he has just had.

(1916)

Facing the Statue of Endymion

In a white chariot drawn by four
milk-white, silver-harnessed mules,
I've arrived at Latmus from Miletus.

I sailed in a purple trireme from Alexandria
for sacred rites—sacrifices and libations—to Endymion.
Look, the statue. Thrilled, I now take in
Endymion's renowned beauty.
My slaves empty baskets of jasmine; auspicious
cheers awaken the pleasures of ancient times.

(1916)

In a Town of Osroene

Around midnight yesterday they brought us
our friend Remon, wounded in a taverna brawl.
Through the windows we had left wide open,
the moon shone on his lovely body on the bed.
We're quite a mix here: Syrian, Greek, Armenian, Mede.
Which is what Remon is. But last night
when the moon shone on his amorous face,
we were reminded of Plato's Charmides.

(1917)

Passage

Things he timidly imagined as a student, have opened
in full view before him. And he cruises, spends all-nighters,
and is led astray. And as is right (for our art),
pleasure revels in his blood, fresh and hot.
Forbidden erotic ecstasy overcomes
his body; and his young limbs
surrender to it.
                And so a simple boy
becomes worth our watching, and for a moment
even he passes through the High World of Poetry—
the boy sensualist, his blood fresh and hot.

(1917)

For Ammonis, Who Died at 29 in 610

Raphael, they have requested you compose
a few lines for the poet Ammonis' epitaph.
Something quite elegant and fine. You can do it,
you're the right one to write as befits
our very own, the poet Ammonis.

For sure, you'll speak about his poems—
but you should speak as well about his beauty,
about his delicate beauty we so loved.

Your Greek is always graceful and melodious.
But now we must have all your artistry.
Our grief and love must pass through a foreign tongue.
Pour your Egyptian feeling into it, this foreign tongue.

Raphael, your verses should be written
to have, you know, something of our life in them,
where the rhythm and every phrase profess
an Alexandrian writes about an Alexandrian.

(1917)

One of Their Gods

When one of them rushed through Seleucia's
center of town round about dusk time
like one of those tall, fabulous looking young men,
his eyes ashine with his incorruptibility,
with his black hair perfumed,
those he encountered stared at him
and asked each other who he was,
a Syrian Greek, maybe, or a stranger.
But those who looked more sharply
got it and got out of his way;
and as he disappeared through the arcades
into the shadows and lights of the night,
making his way to the zone that lives
only after dark on orgies and debauchery
and all kinds of "highs" and lechery,
they wondered which one of Them he was,
and for what questionable pleasure
he'd descended onto Seleucia's streets
from that high and hallowed home of his.

(1917)

In the Evening

In any case they wouldn't have held out long. My years
of experience show me that. But Fate came
rather quickly and put an end to it all.
That beautiful life was brief.
Yet how powerful were its perfumes,
what a wonderful bed we lay upon,
what pleasures we gave our bodies to.

An echo from those days of pleasure,
an echo from those days came to me,
something from the youthful fire in the two of us:
I held a letter in my hands again,
and read it over and over till the light had waned.

Melancholy, I stepped out onto the balcony—
stepped out to change my thoughts at least by seeing
a little something of this beloved city,
a little movement in the streets and shops.

(1917)

To Pleasure

Joy and balm of my life the memory of those hours
when I found and held fast to pleasure as I wanted it.
Joy and balm of my life for me that I recoiled
from delight in any routine acts of love.

(1917)

Gray

Looking at a pale gray opal
I remembered two beautiful gray eyes
that I saw; must have been twenty years ago…

....

We were lovers for a month.
Then he took off, for Smyrna I think,
for a job there, and we never saw each other again.

They'll have lost their look—if he lives—those gray eyes;
that beautiful face will have broken down.

Memory, keep it the way it was.
And, memory, whatever you can of that love,
whatsoever you can, bring back to me tonight.

(1917)

Tomb of Iases

Here I, Iases, lie. All over this great city
the youth most famous for his beauty.
The very wise marveled at me, as did the ordinary
common people. And I enjoyed both equally.

But from the people's taking me for a Narcissus or a Hermes so much,
the excesses beat me down, killed me. Passerby,
if you're an Alexandrian, you will not scold. You know
how fast and furious our life is, how hot it is, pleasure's fullest pitch.

(1917)

In the Month of Athyr

With difficulty I read   this ancient stone.
"L[OR]D JESUS CHRIST."   I can decipher a "SO[U]L."
"IN THE MON[TH] OF ATHYR"   "LEFKIO[S] FELL ASLEEP."
At the mention of years,   "HE LI[VE]D TO THE AGE OF,"
the Kappa Zeta reveals   he was young when he fell asleep.
On a worn away part I can see   "HI[M]...ALEXANDRIAN."
There follow three lines   that are extremely mutilated,
but I can make out a few words—   like "OUR T[EAR]S," "GRIEF,"
then "TEARS" again,   and "MOURNED B[Y] HIS [F]RIENDS."
It seems to me Lefkios   was deeply loved.
In the month of Athyr   Lefkios fell asleep.

(1917)

I've Gazed So Much

I've gazed so much on beauty,
it fills my vision to the brim.

Body's contours. Red lips. Sensual limbs.
Hair as if taken from Greek statues,
always beautiful, even uncombed,
and falling a little over pale foreheads.
Faces of love, just as my poetry
desired them ... in the nights of my youth,
in my nights secretly encountered...

(1917)

Tomb of Ignatius

Here I am not the Cleon once known
in Alexandria (where it's hard to show off)
for my splendid houses, for my gardens,
for my horses and my chariots,
for the diamonds and the silks I dressed in.
Get out! I am not that Cleon:
let his twenty-eight years be erased.
I'm Ignatius, church lector, who took his sweet time
to come around; yet I still lived ten happy months
in the peace and safe keeping of Christ.

(1917)

Days of 1903

I never found them again—that were so quickly lost…
the poetic eyes, the pallid
face… in the street's nightfall….

I never found them again—what I came by wholly through luck,
and so easily gave up,
then later longed for in anguish.
The poetic eyes, the pale face,
those lips I never found again.

(1917)

The Tobacco Shop Window

They stood among many others
near a brightly lighted tobacco shop window.
By chance their glances coupled,
and timidly, tentatively expressed
the illicit desires of their bodies.
Later, a few anxious steps on the sidewalk—
until they smiled and nodded slightly.

And after that the closed carriage…
the sensuous convergence of bodies;
the bonded hands, the bonded lips.

(1917)

Half an Hour

Never made it with you and don't expect
I will. Some talk, a slight move closer,
as in the bar yesterday, nothing more.
A pity, I won't deny. But we artists
now and then by pushing our minds
can—but only for a moment—create
a pleasure that seems almost physical.
That's why in the bar yesterday—with the help
of alcohol's merciful power—I had
a half-hour that was completely erotic.
I think you knew it and
stayed on purpose a little longer.
That was really necessary. Because
with all my imagination and spell of the drinks,
I just had to see your lips,
had to have your body near.

(1917)

Symeon

Yes, I am acquainted with his new poems.
All Beirut is quite taken with them.
I'll read them closely another day.
Today I can't because I'm rather troubled.

He's surely better versed in Greek than Libanios.
But is he better than Meleagros? I don't think so.

Ah, Mebes, we should care about Libanios and books!
What trifles!… Yesterday, Mebes, I came to be—
quite by chance—under Symeon's pillar.

I had slipped in among the Christians
who were silently in prayer and worship
kneeling there. Being no Christian myself,
I did not partake of their serenity—
I shivered all over and suffered,
I shook, agitated and overcome.

Now don't smile: for thirty-five years, just think—
winter, summer, night and day, thirty-five
years to live and bear witness upon a pillar.
Before we were born—I am twenty-nine
and you a bit younger, I guess—
before we were born, imagine that,
Symeon climbed up his pillar
and remained there ever since before God.

I cannot put my mind to work today—
At least, Mebes, better to tell them
that despite what other sophists may say,
I do recognize Lamon
as Syria's premier poet.

(1917)

Caesarion

Partly to verify something about a period,
partly merely to pass the time,
last night I picked up and read a collection
of inscriptions about the Ptolemies.
The profuse praise and flattery
the same for all of them. Each and every one brilliant,
illustrious, mighty, benevolent;
every one of their undertakings most wise.
Speaking of the women in their line, they too,
all the Berenices and Cleopatras, marvelous.

When I succeeded in verifying what I was after
I'd have put back the book if a brief,
trifling mention of King Caesarion
hadn't suddenly caught my eye ….

Ah, there, you've come with that hard to pin down
charm of yours. Only a few lines
about you can be found in history,
so I all the more freely made you up in my mind.
I made you handsome and sensitive.
My art gives your face
a dreamy kindly beauty.
And so fully did I imagine you
that late last night, as my lamp
went out—I deliberately let it go out—
I dared to suppose you entered my room,
you stood, it seemed, in front of me: as if
you were in conquered Alexandria,
pale and weary, perfect in your grief,
still hopeful that they'd take pity on you,
those rogues—who whispered "Too many Caesars."

(1918)

Remember, Body

Body, remember not only how much you were loved,
not only the beds you lay on,
but also those desires that glowed
openly for you in eyes,
and in quavering voices—only to be
thwarted by some chance interference.
Now that that's all in the past
it seems almost as if you also gave
yourself to those desires too—how they glowed,
remember, in those eyes that looked at you,
quavered in the voice for you, remember, body.

(1918)

Tomb of Lanes

The Lanes you loved is not here, Marcus,
in the tomb to which you come to weep and linger hour after hour.
The Lanes you loved you have much closer to you
when shut in at home you look at his portrait,
which preserves something of what was of value in him,
which preserves something of what you loved in him.

Remember, Marcus, how you once brought in
the famous Cyrenian painter from the proconsul's palace,
and how with all his artistic cunning,
the second after he saw your friend, wanted to convince you
he should definitely do him as Hyacinth
(thus the buzz about his portrait would spread).

But your Lanes didn't lend out his beauty so;
and firmly opposed he told him not to depict
in any way Hyacinth, or anyone else,
but Lanes, the son of Rhametichus, an Alexandrian.

(1918)

Getting It

Years of my youth, my sensual life—
how clearly I now see their meaning.

What needless regrets, what vain ....

But I didn't get it then.

During my loose living days of youth
the disposition of my poetry took form,
the scope of my art was laid down.

That's why the regrets were never ever firm.
And my decisions to contain myself, to change
lasted a couple of weeks at the most.

(1918)

Nero's Deadline

Nero was not troubled after he heard
the prophecy from the Delphic Oracle.
"Of seventy-three years let him beware."
He still had time to enjoy himself.
He's thirty years old. The deadline
the god's giving him is more than enough
to address any future dangers.

Now he'll return to Rome a bit tired,
but beautifully tired from that trip,
when he was into pleasure day in day out—
in the theatres, the gardens, the gymns …
Soirées in the cities of Achaea …
Ah, the rapture of naked bodies above all …

Enough about Nero. Meanwhile in Spain Galba
secretly musters and trains his army,
him, an old man of seventy-three.

(1918)

Envoys from Alexandria

For centuries they hadn't seen such beautiful gifts
at Delphi as these sent by the two brothers,
the rival Ptolemaic kings. But now
that they've got them, the priests are worried about the prophecy.
They'll need all their know-how to put it shrewdly,
which of the two, the likes of these two, should be offended.
And they meet in secret at night
and talk over the Lagids' family matters.

But look, the envoys have come back. They take leave.
Returning to Alexandria, they say. And they're not asking
for any oracle. And the priests are pleased to hear this
(it's understood they'll keep the splendid gifts),
but they're extremely taken aback,
without an inkling what this sudden loss of interest means.
For they don't know the envoys got some grave news the day before.
The oracle was given in Rome; the divvying-up was determined there.

(1918)

Aristoboulus

The palace weeps, the king weeps,
King Herod grieves inconsolably,
the whole city weeps for Aristoboulus
who accidentally drowned so senselessly
while playing with his friends in the water.

And when the news of this spreads,
when it circulates in Syria,
even many Greeks will be saddened,
as many poets and sculptors will mourn,
because Aristoboulus was well-known to them,
though never had they even come close to imagining
a young man's beauty such as this boy's;
Antioch was never worthy of having a statue of a god
to compare with this child of Israel.

The first princess wails and weeps,
his mother, the greatest of Jewish women.
Alexandra wails and weeps for this disaster.—
But as soon as she's alone her agony transforms.
She roars, rages, swears, speaks curses.
How they fooled her! How they duped her!
How they had their way at last!
They destroyed the house of the Hasmoneans.
How that nefarious king has succeeded,
that conniving, corrupt scoundrel.
How he succeeded. What a fiendish plot
for even Miriam not to catch wind of it.
If Miriam had, if she'd suspected anything,
she'd have found a way to save her brother;
she's queen after all, she could have done something.
How they must be secretly exulting and rejoicing now,
those malicious ones, Cyprus and Salome,
those filthy women, Cyprus and Salome.—
And to be powerless, and forced

to pretend she believes their lies;
to be unable to go before the people,
to go and shout it to the Jews,
to say, to say how the murder was committed.

(1918)

In the Harbor

A young man of twenty-eight, Emis arrived
in this Syrian harbor on a ship from Tinos
with the purpose of learning to sell perfume.
He became ill during the passage, however,
and died when he disembarked. His pauper's
burial took place here. A few hours before he died,
he muttered the words "home" and "very old parents."
But nobody knew who they were,
or his country in this vast panhellenic world.
That's better. Because this way,
though he lies dead in this harbor,
his parents will always hope he's alive.

(1918)

Aemilianus Monae, Alexandrian

A. D. 628-655

With words, appearance, and behaviors
I'll make a first rate suit of armor;
and thus I will confront evil people
without any fear or weakness.

They'll want to hurt me. But none will know
of those who approach me
where my wounds sit, my vulnerable spots,
beneath the lies that will cover me.—

Boastful words of Aemilianus Monae.
I wonder if he ever did make that suit of armor?
In any event, he didn't wear it long.
At age twenty-seven, he died in Sicily.

(1918)

Since Nine O'Clock

Half past twelve. Time's passed quickly
since nine o'clock when I lit the lamp
and sat down here. I sat without reading,
without talking. To whom would I talk
all by myself in this house.

The image of my youthful body,
since nine o'clock when I lit the lamp,
came and found me and reminded me
of closed, redolent rooms
and of past pleasure—what daring pleasure!
And it also brought to mind
streets that are now unrecognizable,
lively nightclubs that have closed down,
theatres and cafés from once upon a time.

The image of my youthful body
came and also brought me things of sadness:
the family in mourning, separations,
my close ones' feelings, feelings
of the dead so lightly regarded.

Half past twelve. How time flies.
Half past twelve. How the years go by.

(1918)

Below the House

Walking yesterday in a neighborhood
on the outskirts of town, I passed below the house
I went to when I was very young.
It was there Eros took over my body
with his awesome might.

And yesterday
as I passed along the old road,
love's magic immediately beautified
the shops, the sidewalks, the stones,
the walls, balconies, and windows;
nothing there remained unsightly.

And as I stood, looking at the door,
and stood, and lingered below the house,
my entire being exuded
bottled up sensual emotion.

(1918)

The Next Table

He must be just about twenty-two years old.
And yet I am certain that, nearly an equal
number of years ago, I enjoyed that very same body.

This is by no means an erotic transport.
And I entered the casino a little while ago,
so I haven't even had time to drink much.
I enjoyed that same body.

And if I don't remember where—my forgetfulness
doesn't really matter.

Ah, there, now that he's sitting at the next table,
I recognize every move he makes--and under his clothes
I see again those beloved naked limbs.

(1918)

The Afternoon Sun

This is the room, I know it well.
Now it and next door are for rent
as business offices. The entire house,
offices for realtors, businessmen, companies.

Ah, this room, so familiar.

Here, near the door was the sofa,
in front of it a Turkish rug;
near by, the shelf with two yellow vases.
To the right—no, opposite, a wardrobe with a mirror.
In the middle, the table where he wrote;
and the three large wicker chairs.
Beside the window was the bed
where we loved each other so many times.

They still must be around somewhere, poor old things.

Beside the window was the bed
the reach of the afternoon sun divided in half.

...At four o'clock one afternoon, we were separating
for just a week... And oh,
that week became forever.

(1919)

Comes to Reside

It must have been one o'clock at night
or one-thirty.

    In a corner of a tavern,
behind a wooden partition.
Except for the two of us the place was completely empty.
A kerosene lamp barely lighted it.
The waiter, awake too long, slept by the door.

No one could see us. And besides
we were so carried away
we were incapable of taking precautions.

Our clothes half opened--we were dressed lightly
because heavenly July was so hot.

Carnal pleasure between
half opened clothes,
quick baring of flesh—whose image
spans these twenty-six years, and now
comes to reside in this poetry.

(1919)

Of the Jews (50 A.D.)

Painter and poet, runner and discus-thrower,
handsome as Endymion, Ianthes, son of Antonius.
From a family affiliated with the Synagogue.

"My most honorable days are those
when I quit the sensual quest,
when I forsake lovely and exacting Hellenism,
with its prevailing attachment
to perfectly made and perishable white limbs.
And I become the man I'd want
to remain forever: son of the Jews, the holy Jews."

Quite a fervent affirmation this.
"To remain forever of the Jews, the holy Jews—"

But he remained nothing of the kind.
The Hedonism and Art of Alexandria
retained him as their devoted child.

(1919)

Imenus

"…to be loved even more
the sensual delight realized morbidly and with depravity;
rarely finding the body that feels delight the way it wants it to—
that, morbidly and with depravity, rouses
an erotic intensity that sound health cannot know…"

Fragment from a letter
by the young Imenus (a patrician) well-known
in Syracuse for his dissipation,
during the dissipated times of Michael the Third.

(1919)

Aboard Ship

A good likeness, for sure, this small
portrait in pencil of him.

Quickly done on the ship's deck
one magical afternoon.
The Ionian Sea all around us.

A good likeness. Yet I recall him as handsomer.
He was almost afflicted with sensitivity,
and that lit up his expression.
He seems handsomer to me
now that my soul summons him out of Time.

Out of Time. All these things are very old—
the sketch, the ship, the afternoon.

(1919)

Of Demetrius Soter (162-150 B.C.)

Every one of his expectations turned out wrong!

He imagined himself performing deeds of renown,
which put an end to the humiliation that had oppressed
his homeland ever since the battle of Magnesia.
That Syria would once again become a powerful state,
with her armies, with her fleets,
with great fortresses and wealth.

He'd suffered, become embittered in Rome
when he perceived in the speech of friends,
the young men of the great families,
with all the tact and good manners
they showed him, the son
of King Seleucus Philopater—
when he perceived that all this only concealed
contempt for the Hellenizing dynasties:
they were in decline, ill-suited for serious work,
quite incapable of ruling their people.
He drew himself apart, indignant, and swore
things were not at all what they thought;
see here, he has the will;
he'll put up the fight, he'll take action, he'll uphold it.

If he could only find a way to get to the East,
succeed in getting out of Italy—
then all of this strength of soul
he has and all of his fury
he'd impart to the people.

If only he could be in Syria!
He was such a little boy when he left his country
he has only hazy memories of the place.
But he always kept thinking of it
as if it were something sacred to be approached with reverence,

a mirage of a beautiful place, a vision
of Greek cities and harbors.—

And now?
      Now despair and anguish.
Those young men in Rome were right.
It's impossible to sustain those dynasties
the Macedonian Conquest had produced.

No matter: he had tried hard,
fought as much as he could.
And in his black disillusion,
there's only one thing he can reckon
with pride, that even in failure
he shows the same invincible valor to all the world.

As for the rest—dreams and wasted efforts.
This Syria—it hardly resembles his homeland,
It's the land of Herakleides and Valas.

(1919)

The Bandaged Shoulder

He said he'd bumped into a wall or fallen down.
But it's likely there was another reason
for his injured and bandaged shoulder.

With a sudden, outstretched movement
to reach a shelf and take down
some photographs he wanted to look at closely,
the bandage came loose and a little blood trickled.

I wrapped up the shoulder again, and took my time
in the binding; he felt no pain
and I enjoyed looking at the blood. A thing
that belonged to my love, that blood.

When he left, I found in front of his chair
a blood-stained rag from the dressing,
a rag meant to be tossed right into the trash;
and I raised it to my lips,
and pressed it there a long time—
blood of my love upon my lips.

(1919)

If Dead Then

"Where did he go away to, where did the Sage disappear?
After his many miracles,
the renown of his teachings
which spread to so many nations
he suddenly went into hiding and nobody found out
for sure what became of him
(nor did anyone ever see his grave).
Some put out the word that he died in Ephesus.
Yet Damis wrote nothing about that;
Damis writes nothing about the death of Apollonius.
Others said he disappeared from sight in Lindos.
Or maybe the story's true
that he ascended to heaven in Crete
at Dictynna's ancient shrine.—
But then we have that miraculous,
that supernatural appearance of his
to a young student at Tyana.—
Maybe it isn't time yet for him to return
to show up in the world again;
or maybe, transfigured, he goes about
among us unrecognized. But he will show up again
as he was, teaching what's upright, and then for sure
he'll reinstate the worship of our gods,
and our elegant Hellenic ceremonies."

This is how he fantasized in his squalid lodging—
after reading Philostratus'
"On Apollonius of Tyana"—
one of the few pagans,
the very few who were left. Otherwise—an unremarkable
and faint of heart man—outwardly
making like a Christian and going to church, too.
It was the time the aged Justin
ruled with utmost piety,

and Alexandria, a god-fearing city,
abhorred wretched idolators.

(1920)

Young Men of Sidon (400 A.D.)

The actor they brought in to amuse them
also recited some choice epigrams.

The chamber opened on to the garden
and wore a mild scent of flowers
that mingled with the fragrances
of the five perfumed young Sidonians.

Some Meleagros, Krinagoras, and Rhianos were read.
But when the actor declaimed
"Here lies Aeschylus, son of Euphorion, an Athenian—"
(perhaps emphasizing more than necessary
"his renowned valor" and "the grove of Marathon"),
a high spirited youth, fanatically into literature,
sprang up suddenly and cried out:

"Oh, I don't care for that quatrain.
Such expressions seem rather faint-hearted.
Give—say I—all you have to your work,
all your care, and keep your work in mind
even during hardships, even as your time winds down.
This is what I expect and demand of you.
And not that you totally overlook
the brilliant art of your tragedies,
the *Agamemnon*, the wonderful *Prometheus*,
the characters of Orestes and Cassandra,
the *Seven Against Thebes*—you offer instead as your memorial
only that among the mass of rank and file soldiers
you too fought against the Persians Datis and Artaphernes."

(1920)

So They'll Come—

A single candle will do.   Its faint light
will be just right,   will be more tender
for when they come,   when Love's Shades come.

A single candle will do.   The room tonight
needn't have much light.   In a deep reverie
and suggestive mood,   and with the light very low—
thus in my reverie   I'll frame a vision
so they will come,   so Love's Shades will come.

(1920)

Darius

Phernazes the poet is working
on the major part of his epic.
All about how Darius, son of Hystaspes,
took over the Persian kingdom. (From him
our glorious king's descended,
Mithridates, Dionysus and Eupator). But here
some philosophy is necessary; he must figure out
the feelings Darius must have experienced:
perhaps arrogance and intoxication; but no—rather
something like grasping the vanities of grandeur.
The poet thinks hard about this problem.

But his servant interrupts him when he
rushes in and announces news of great impact.
The war with the Romans has begun.
Most of our army has crossed the borders.

The poet stands speechless. What a disaster!
 Now how can our glorious king,
Mithridates, Dionysus and Eupator,
become occupied with Greek poems.
In the middle of a war—can you imagine, Greek poems.

Phernazes agonizes. Rotten luck!
Just when he was certain to make his mark
with his "Darius," and to shut up for good
those envious carping critics of his.
What a setback, what a setback to his agenda.

And if it's only a setback, well all right.
But let's see how safe we are here
in Amisos. Not an especially well fortified town.
The Romans are a most frightful enemy.
Could we give them a good fight,
we Cappadocians? Could that ever happen?

Are we any competition for the legions?
Great gods, Asia's protectors, come to our aid—

But in the midst of all his agitation and the turmoil,
the poetic idea persistently comes and goes—
of course, it had to be arrogance and intoxication;
arrogance and intoxication that Darius had felt.

(1920)

Anna Comnena

Anna Comnena laments her widowhood
in the prologue to her *Alexiad*.

Her soul's in a dizzy spin. "And my eyes
are awash," she tells us, "with streams
of tears… Alas for the waves" of her life,
"alas for the upheavals." Affliction burns her
"to her bones and marrow and the cleaving of her soul."

But the truth would seem that this
power-hungry woman knew but one harsh grief;
she experienced only one deep hurt
(even if she won't admit it) this imperious Greek woman,
that she failed, for all her know-how,
to win the throne; in fact, it was snatched
virtually out of her hands by the insolent John.

(1920)

A Byzantine Noble, In Exile, Versifying

So let the lightweights call me a lightweight.
About serious matters I've always been
most studious. And I must insist
that nobody is more knowledgeable than I
on the Fathers, the Scriptures, or the Synodal Canons.
Botaniates, whenever in doubt,
whenever in difficulty with ecclesiastical issues,
used to consult me, me first.
But exiled here (no thanks to that malevolent
Irene Ducas), and bored to death,
it would by no means be unreasonable to amuse
myself by making six- and eight-line verses—
to amuse myself with mythological stories
about Hermes, Apollo, and Dionysus,
or the heroes of Thessaly and the Peloponnese;
and to compose in the strictest iambics,
such as—if you'll permit me to say—the literati
of Constantinople have no idea how to compose.
This strictness, it could be, is the reason for their reproach.

(1921)

Their Beginning

The fulfillment of their illicit pleasure
has come about. They get up from the mattress
and quickly dress in silence.
They leave the house separately, furtively,
and as they walk a little anxiously down the street,
it seems they suspect something about them betrays
what kind of bed they fell upon a while ago.

But what a gain for the artist's life.
Tomorrow, the day after, years later, the strong lines
will be written that had their beginning here.

(1921)

The Favor of Alexander Valas

Oh, I'm not bothered that a wheel
on my chariot broke and I didn't win that joke of a race.
I'll spend the night with good wines
and lovely roses all around. Antioch belongs to me.
I'm the most celebrated young man here.
Valas' weakness I am, his idol.
You'll see, tomorrow they'll say the race wasn't on the up and up.
(Now if I were totally tasteless and pressed for it on the sly—
those toadies would even have awarded first place to my crip of a chariot).

(1921)

Melancholy of Jason Cleander, Poet in Commagene, 595 A. D.

The aging of my body and my beauty
is a wound from a savage knife.
To this I am hardly resigned.
I resort to you, Art of Poetry,
because you know something about drugs:
shots at numbing the pain, in Imagination and Words.

It's a wound from a savage knife.—
Bring your nepenthe, Art of Poetry,
that makes for—a little while—no feeling in the wound.

(1921)

Demaratus

His subject, "The Character of Demaratus,"
which Porphyry proposed during a conversation,
was roughed out by the young sophist this way
(he planned to amplify it rhetorically later).

"First a courtier to King Darius,
then later to King Xerxes;
and now with Xerxes and his armed forces,
Demaratus will finally be vindicated.

"A great injustice had been done him.
He *was* Ariston's son. His boldfaced
enemies had paid off the oracle.
And as if it weren't enough to deprive him of his kingship,
then when he finally backed down, and decided
to live in resignation as a private person,
they had to insult him before the people,
they had to publicly humiliate him at the festival.

"So then he serves Xerxes with much zeal.
Along with the great Persian army
he will come back again to Sparta;
and king as he was before, how quickly
he'll get rid of him, how he'll bring down
that schemer Leotychides.

"And the days pass for him full of cares;
giving advice to the Persians, explaining
what they have to do to conquer Greece.

"Lots to worry about, lots to think about and because of that
Demaratus' days are so wearisome;
Lots to worry about, lots to think about and because of that
Demaratus can't find a single moment of joy;
because what he's feeling isn't joy

(it isn't; he won't admit it;
how can he call it joy? his misfortune has reached its limit)
now that things make it clear to him
that the Greeks will come out the winners."

(1921)

I Brought to Art

I sit in reverie.   I brought to Art
desires and sentiments—   some half-seen
faces or contours;   some shaky memories
of fumbled love affairs.   Let me submit to it.
It knows how to shape   the Form of Beauty;
almost imperceptibly   completing life,
fusing impressions,   fusing the days.

(1921)

From the School of the Renowned Philosopher

For two years he was a student of Ammonius Saccas;
but he grew weary of both philosophy and Saccas.

Next, he tried out politics.
But he gave it up. The Sub-Prefect was a fool,
and those around him bureaucratic officious boneheads;
their Greek invariably barbaric, the miserable losers.

The Church piqued
his curiosity: to be baptized
and pass as a Christian. But he changed
his mind pretty fast. It would certainly make for trouble
with his parents, openly pagan;
and they'd promptly put a stop—perish the thought—
to their very liberal allowance.

But he just had to do something. He started to hang out
at the most depraved houses in Alexandria,
every secret haunt of debauchery.

In this his luck had been good to him:
it had given him over-the-top good looks.
And he delighted in this divine gift.

His handsome looks would last for at least
another ten years. And after that—
he might go back again to Saccas.
And if in the meantime the old man had died,
he'd go to another philosopher or sophist;
someone suitable always turns up.

Or in the end, going back to politics
would be a possibility—a laudable observance
of his family traditions,
duty to one's country and other high-sounding stuff like that.

(1921)

Craftsman of Wine Bowls

On this wine bowl   of pure silver—
made for the house   of Herakleides,
where grand style   and good taste rule—
observe the elegant flowers,   streams and thyme,
in whose midst I set   a handsome young man,
naked, amorous,   with one leg still
dangling in the water.—   O memory, I prayed
you'd be my best assistant   in making
the young man's face I loved   the way it was.
A great difficulty   this proved because
about fifteen years   have passed since the day
he fell, a soldier,   in the defeat at Magnesia.

(1921)

Those Who Fought for the Achaean League

You brave men who fought and fell with glory;
never fearing those who'd won battles everywhere.
Blameless are you, even if Diaeus and Critolaus were at fault.
When the Greeks will want to boast,
"Such are the men our nation begets," they'll say
about you. So wonderful the praise for you will be.—

Written in Alexandria by an Achaean;
in the seventh year of Ptolemy Lathyros.

(1922)

To Antiochus Epiphanes

The young Antiochian   said to the king,
"My heart pounds   with a precious hope;
the Macedonians are back,   Antiochus Epiphanes,
the Macdeonians back   in the great struggle.
Just let them win—   and I'll give anyone who wants them
the lion and the horses,   the Pan of coral,
and the elegant palace,   the gardens of Tyre,
and everything else you've given me,   Antiochus Epiphanes."

Maybe the king   was moved a bit.
But he remembered on the spot   his father and brother,
and did not respond.   An eavesdropper could
repeat something.—   Moreover, as expected,
quickly came at Pydna   the horrific closure.

(1922)

In an Antique Book

In an antique book—about a hundred years old—
forgotten between its pages,
I found an unsigned watercolor.
It must have been the work of a mighty artist.
It was entitled, "Presentation of Love."

"Love for the Compleat Sensualist" would have been more apt.

Because it was obvious as you looked at the work
(it was easy to get the artist's idea)
that the young man in the picture had not been cut out
for those who love in more or less healthy ways,
staying within the limits of what can be
allowed—with his deeply dark chestnut eyes,
with that exquisitely beautiful face of his,
the beauty of perverse attractions,
with those incomparable lips that bear
sensual delight to the beloved body,
with those super limbs of his framed for beds
that current morality calls shameless.

(1922)

In Despair

He's lost him altogether.   And now keeps on seeking
in the lips of every   new lover
those lips of his;   in pairing off with each
new lover   he seeks to be taken in
that he's the same young man,   that he gives himself to him.

He's lost him altogether,   as if he'd never been.
Because he wanted—that one said—   to save himself
from the stigmatized,   the sick sensuality;
from the stigmatized,   the shameful sensuality.
There was still time—   as he said—to save himself.

He's lost him altogether,   as if he'd never been.
Through fantasies,   through illusions
from the lips of other youths   he seeks the lips of him;
he yearns to feel   his kind of love again.

(1923)

Julian Seeing Indifference

"Marking, then, that there is great indifference
among us toward the gods"—he says with a severe air.
Indifference. But then what did he expect?
Let him work, as much as he wants, in religious organizing,
let him write, as much as he wants, to the high priest of Galatia,
or to others of that sort, exhorting and directing.
His friends were not Christians;
that's for sure. But for all that they couldn't
play as he did (having been raised Christian)
with a novel religious system,
absurd both in its conception and practice.
They were, after all, Greeks. Nothing in excess, Augustus.

(1923)

Epitaph of Antiochus, King of Commagene

After she returned, grief-stricken, from his funeral,
the sister of the temperate and tranquil living,
the deeply learned Antiochus, the King
of Commagene, wanted an epitaph for him.
And the Ephesian sophist Callistratus—
often a resident of the small state of Commagene,
a happily and frequently hosted guest
in the royal household—
composed it, as advised by Syrian courtiers,
and sent it on to the aged lady.

"May the fame of the benevolent King Antiochus
be duly commemorated, O Commagenians.
He was a provident ruler of the country.
He lived a life of justice, wisdom, bravery.
He lived a life moreover that was best of all, Hellenic—
mankind owns no quality more precious;
anything beyond that is territory of the gods."

(1923)

Theatre of Sidon (A.D. 400)

Son of an honest citizen—   most important, a handsome
young boy of the theatre,   alluring in diverse ways,
I now and then compose   in the Greek language
extremely audacious verses,   which I circulate
strictly under the table, you understand—   gods! let them not be seen
by those who drably garbed   blather about morals—
verses about pleasures   of a choice kind,
that trails after a love   that is futile and damned.

(1923)

Julian in Nicomedia

Pointless and dangerous doings.
The paeans to Greek ideals.

The theurgic incidents and visits to pagan
temples. This enthusiasm for the ancient gods.

The frequent colloquies with Chrysanthius.
The theories of the—also very sharp—philosopher Maximus.

With this result. Gallus exhibits great
anxiety. Constantius is somewhat suspicious.

His advisors were not all that judicious.
This story's been overworked—says Mardonius,

and the buzz has to be definitely stopped.
Julian goes back to being Lector

at the church in Nicomedia,
where in full voice and with deep

reverence he reads the Holy Scriptures,
and the people admire his Christian piety.

(1924)

Before Time Could Change Them

They were so very sad   at their parting.
They hadn't wanted it;   it was circumstances.
Life's necessities   compelled one of them
to go far away—   New York or Canada.
Their love, of course,   was not what it had been before;
the attraction   had cooled gradually,
the attraction   had cooled a lot.
But to separate,   that's not what they wanted.
It was circumstances.—   Or maybe Destiny
came on like an artist   separating them now
before their feeling turned off,   before Time could change them:
each one for the other   to remain forever
the twenty-four year old   beautiful young boy.

(1924)

He Came to Read

He came to read. Two or three books
lie open, books by historians and poets.
But after barely ten minutes of reading,
he let them go. He's half asleep
on the sofa. He's totally devoted to books—
but he is twenty-three years old, and very good looking;
and this afternoon Eros passed through
his most perfect flesh, through his lips.
Through his utterly lovely flesh
the ardor of Eros spread;
with no asinine shame for the shape that pleasure took.

(1924)

31 B.C. in Alexandria

From his hamlet near the city boundary,
still covered with dust from the journey

the peddler arrives. And "Incense!" and "Gum!"
"The finest olive oil!" "For your hair, perfume!"

he hawks in the streets. But with the huge roar,
and the music and parades, impossible for him to be heard.

The throng shoves him, drags him, and knocks him about.
And when, all confused, "What's this craziness about?" he asks,

one of them throws him the line from the palace,
biggest of lies—in Greece, Antony's victorious.

(1924)

John Cantacuzenus Triumphs

He looks at the fields that still belong to him
with the wheat, the livestock, the fruit-bearing
trees. And a little further on his ancestral home,
full of clothes, expensive furnishings, and silverware.

They're going to take it from him—Jesus Christ!—
they're going to take it now.

Could be Cantacuzenus will take pity on him
if he goes and throws himself at his feet. He's forbearing, they say,
very forbearing. But those around him? But the army?—
Or should he prostrate himself and complain to Lady Irene?

Stupid! To get tangled up in Anna's party—
damn Lord Andronicus for ever marrying her.
Have we ever seen anything good come
of her behavior, ever seen any humanity?
By now even the Franks no longer respect her.
Her schemes were laughable, all of her arrangements silly.
While they were a menace to everyone from the City,
Cantacuzenus smashed them, Lord John just smashed them.

And to think he had a notion to take Lord John's
side! And would have done it. And he'd be happy now,
still a great noble, and on solid footing,
if the bishop hadn't swayed him at the final moment,
with his sacerdotal imposition,
with his end to end erroneous information,
with his promises, and claptrap.

(1924)

Temethus, Antiochian: 400 A.D.

Verses by young Temethus   the lovelorn.
Entitled "Emonides"—   beloved partner
of Antiochus Epiphanes;   a great looking
young man from Samosata.   But if the verses turn out
passionate, emotional   it's because Emonides
(from another   much older period:
year one hundred thirty-seven   of the Greek reign!—
a little earlier perhaps)   was added to the poem
only as a name;   a fitting one nonetheless.
The poem articulates   one love of Temethus,
beautiful and worthy of him.   We the initiates,
his intimate friends,   we the initiates
know for whom   those verses were written.
The clueless Antiochians   read: Emonides.

(1925)

Of Colored Glass

I'm quite touched by a single detail
in the coronation at Blachernae of John Cantacuzenus
and Irene, daughter of Andronicus Asan.
Inasmuch as they had very few precious stones
(our hapless state was extremely poor)
they wore artificial ones. A pile of glass pieces,
red, green, or blue. In my view
there's nothing shameful or undignified
about those little pieces
of colored glass. To the contrary, they seem
but a sad protestation
against the unfair sorry state of those being crowned.
They are symbols of what they ought to have,
of what was without question right for them to have
at the coronation of a Lord John Cantacuzenus
and a Lady Irene, daughter of Andronicus Asan.

(1925)

In the Twenty-fifth Year of His Life

He goes regularly to the taverna
where they had met the month before.
He made inquiries, but they had nothing to tell him.
From what they said, he understood that he had met
a completely unknown individual,
one of the many unknown, questionable
young sorts who happened by there.
He still goes regularly to the taverna, at night,
and sits and looks in the direction of the door,
looks in the door's direction until he's worn out.
Perhaps he'll come in. Perhaps tonight he'll come.

He does this for almost three weeks.
His mind becomes sick with lust.
The kisses linger on his mouth.
He suffers in all his flesh unrelieved longing.
The touch of that other body is still on him.
He wants to be reunited with it.

He does not want to betray himself, of course.
But sometimes he's almost indifferent.
Besides, he knows what he's getting into,
he's made up his mind. It's not unlikely this life of his
will lead him into a ruinous scandal.

(1925)

On an Italian Shore

Cemos, son of Menedorus,   a young Italiote,
passes through life   just partying;
like most of the young men   in Magna Graecia
accustomed to being raised   in a very rich way.

But today he's too,   despite his nature,
preoccupied and gloomy.   Near the quay,
in acute distress   he watches them unload
the ships with the spoils   from the Peloponnese.

Greek booty: the haul from Corinth.

Ah, today for sure   it's just not right,
not at all possible   for the young Italiote
to have any desire   to party.

(1925)

In the Boring Village

In the boring village where he works—
a clerk, a very young one,
in a shop—biding his time
till another two three months go by,
another two three months for business to slow down,
so he can take off for the city and throw himself
straight into the action and good times;
in the boring village where he's biding his time—
he dropped onto his bed tonight overcome with desire,
his youth ignited with bodily passion,
all of his lovely youth into an exquisite intensity.
And pleasure enters in his sleep; right in
his sleep he sees and gets the face and flesh he wanted....

(1925)

Apollonius of Tyana in Rhodes

Apollonius was discussing
proper learning and education
with a young man who was building
a luxury home in Rhodes. "When I enter a temple,"
the Tyanian said in the end, "I'd much
prefer to see even in a small one
a statue made of ivory and gold
rather than a cheap one of clay in a large one."—

The "clay" and the "cheap;" so repulsive:
the kind of con that even now dupes some
(who have not been well-trained). The clay and the cheap.

(1925)

Kleitos' Illness

Kleitos, an appealing
young man, about twenty-three years old—
with a superb education, with uncommon Greek learning—
is seriously ill. He was stricken by the fever
that mowed down Alexandria this year.

The fever found him already morally beat,
agonizing over his partner, a young actor,
who ceased to love or want him.

He is seriously ill, and his parents are in distress.

An old woman servant who reared him
is also shaken up over Kleitos' life.
In her horrific anxiety
there comes to mind an idol she worshiped
as a child, before she arrived there as a servant,
at the home of prominent Christians, and became a Christian herself.
In secrecy she brings cakes, wine, and honey.
She brings them before the idol. She chants whichever parts
of prayers she can remember: random bits and pieces. The dimwit
doesn't get it that the miserable demon could care less
if a Christian recovers or not.

(1926)

In a Township in Asia Minor

The report about the result of the naval battle at Actium,
was certainly unexpected.
But there's no need to re-write the document.
Only the name need be changed. Instead, there
in the last lines, "Liberating the Romans
from the disastrous Octavian,
that parody of a Caesar,"
we now insert, "Liberating the Romans
from the disastrous Antony...."
The entire text matches up beautifully.

"To the most glorious victor,
incomparable in every military pursuit,
admirable for his great political feats,
on whose behalf the township fervently prayed
for Antony's triumph"
here, as we said, the swap: "for Caesar's triumph,
regarded as the finest gift of Zeus—
to the mighty protector of the Greeks,
who graciously honors the Greek ethos,
who is beloved in every Greek land,
who is most worthy of the highest praise,
and whose deeds should be related in full
in the Greek language in verse and in prose;
in the *Greek language*, the bearer of fame,"
et cetera, et cetera. It all matches up superbly.

(1926)

Priest at the Serapeum

The good old man my father,
whose love for me never changed;
the good old man my father I mourn
who died day before yesterday, just before dawn.

Jesus Christ, the commandments
of your most holy church to keep
in my every act, in my every word,
in my every thought is my endeavor
every day. And from all who deny you
I turn away.—But now I mourn;
I grieve, Christ, for my father
though he was—horrible to say—
priest at the accursed Serapeum.

(1926)

In the Dives—

In the dives   and whorehouses
of Beirut I wallow now.   Didn't want to stay
in Alexandria,   Tamides left me;
took off with the son   of the Governor to come by
a Nile villa,   a big house in town.
Wouldn't be right for me   to stay in Alexandria.—
In the dives   and whorehouses
of Beirut I wallow now.   A cheap, debased
low life I lead.   One thing saves me,
like singular beauty,   like a fragrance
that sticks to my skin,   and that's the two years
Tamides was all mine,   loveliest of young men,
all mine and not for a house   or a villa on the Nile.

(1926)

A Great Procession of Priests and Laymen

A procession of priests and laymen,
with all vocations represented,
winds through the streets, squares, and gates
of the celebrated city of Antioch.
At the head of this stately procession
a handsome youth, dressed all in white, holds
the Cross in uplifted hands,
our strength and our hope, the holy Cross.
The pagans, of late so very haughty,
now retiring and timid hurriedly
withdraw from the procession.
Keep away from us, may they always keep away from us
(as long as they don't renounce their error). Onward
the holy Cross. To every quarter
in which Christians live in godliness
it brings consolation and joy:
they come out, these devoted ones, on the steps of their houses
and brimming with jubilation revere it—
the strength, the salvation of the universe, the Cross.—

This is an annual Christian holiday.
But today, you see, it's consummated more conspicuously.
At last the empire has been saved.
The sacrilegious, the abominable
Julian reigns no more.

Let us pray for the most pious Jovian.

(1926)

Sophist Leaving Syria

Notable sophist   now that you're leaving Syria
and plan to write   about Antioch,
it would be worth your while   to mention Mebes in your work.
Mebes the famous   who is indisputably
the most beautiful   most beloved young man
in all Antioch.   Not one of the other
youths in that life-style,   not a single one is paid
as dearly as he.   To have Mebes
for only two, three days   they'll often give him
up to a hundred staters.—   I said, in Antioch;

but also in Alexandria,   and even in Rome,
you'll not find a young man   desirable as Mebes.

(1926)

Julian and the Antiochians

> *The letter Chi, the citizens say, and the letter Kappa*
> *never harmed the city... Finding interpreters*
> *....we learned that these are the initial letters of names,*
> *the first of Christ and the second of Constantius.*
> —Julian, *Misopogon* (The Beard-Hater)

Was it ever possible for them to give up
their lovely way of life, the rich array
of their daily amusements; their brilliant
theatre which begot a union of Art
and the erotic urgings of the flesh!

Immoral to a point—and maybe even more so—
they were for sure. But they had the satisfaction that their life
was the *talk of the town* life of Antioch,
pure sensual pleasure, in absolute good taste.

To renounce all this, to look after what already?

His wind-bagging about the false gods,
his tedious self-promotions;
his infantile fear of the theatre;
his graceless prudery; his ridiculous beard.

O sure they preferred the Chi,
O sure they preferred the Kappa; a hundred times and counting.

(1926)

Anna Dalassene

In the golden bull Alexius Comnenus issued
to honor his mother with distinction,
the exceedingly intelligent Lady Anna Dalassene—
noteworthy for her deeds and her character—
there can be found many laudatory sayings:
here let us bring up from among these
a single beautiful, noble phrase,
"Neither 'mine' nor 'thine,' those chilly words, ever passed her lips."

(1927)

Days of 1896

He'd become thoroughly disgraced.   An erotic bent of his,
utterly transgressive   and contemned
(innate for all that)   was the cause:
society was   prudish to the max.
He'd gradually lost   the little money he had;
his social station was next to go,   and then his reputation.
He was almost thirty   without ever lasting a full
year in a job,   at least one that's recognizable.
Now and then he'd make   his pocket money
as a go-between   in disreputable affairs.
He ended up the type   who if seen with you
a lot, was likely   to compromise you greatly.

But that's not all.   That wouldn't be fair.
The memory of his good looks   deserves better.
There's another point of view   regarded from which
he appears likeable;   appears a simple, authentic
child of love,   who recklessly set
above his honor   and reputation
the pure pleasure   of his pure body.

Above his reputation?   But society, which was
extremely prudish,   judged stupidly.

(1927)

Two Young Men, 23 to 24 Years Old

He was in the café since ten-thirty.
Waiting for him to show up any minute.
Midnight went—and he was still waiting for him.
One-thirty came; the café was
almost completely empty.
He got tired of reading newspapers
from end to end. Of his three miserable shillings
only one remained: waiting for so long
he'd spent the others on coffees and cognac.
He'd smoked all of his cigarettes.
So much waiting around had exhausted him. Because
he was alone that way for so many hours
troubling thoughts began to take him by surprise
about the loose life he was leading.

But as soon as he saw his friend come in—at once
his weariness, his boredom, his worries disappeared.

His friend brought an unexpected bit of news.
He'd won sixty pounds gambling.

Their handsome faces, their exquisite youth,
the sensitive love they shared,
were refreshed, enlivened, invigorated
by the sixty pounds from the gambling.

And now all joy and vigor, excited and beautiful
they went—not to their respectable families' houses
(where they were, in any case, no longer welcome):
to a familiar and very special
house of debauchery they went and asked for
a bedroom and expensive drinks, and they drank again.

And when the expensive drinks were gone,
and it was almost four o'clock,
happy, they gave themselves to love.

(1927)

Greek Since Ancient Times

Antioch takes pride   in her splendid buildings,
and her beautiful streets;   in her marvelous
surrounding countryside,   and in her great
multitude of inhabitants.   She takes pride in being
the seat of glorious kings,   and in her artists
and the sages she has,   and in her super rich
and canny merchants.   But most incomparable
of all, Antioch   takes pride in being a polis
since ancient times;   a sister to Argos:
through that Ione,   founded by Argive
colonists in honor   of the daughter of Inachus.

(1927)

Days of 1901

What was the distinctive thing about him,
that for all his dissolute ways
and his extensive sexual experience,
for all that his habitual
postures accorded with his age,
there were moments—very rarely
of course—when his flesh gave
the impression that it was virtually untried.

His twenty-nine year old beauty,
assayed so much by pleasure,
at times reminded one oddly enough
of a youth who—rather awkwardly—yields
his innocent body to love for the first time.

(1927)

You Didn't Understand

About our religious beliefs—
the empty-headed Julian said, "I read, I understood,
I condemned." He supposed he'd annihilated us
with that "condemned" of his, the buffoon.

Such wisecracks leave us Christians cold.
"You read, but you didn't understand; had you understood,
you wouldn't have condemned," we snapped back.

(1928)

A Young Man, Devoted to the Art of the Word— in His Twenty-Fourth Year

"Work with as much as you've got now, mind.—"
A one-sided passion is using him up.
He's in a state of exasperation.
He kisses the beloved face every day,
his hands always on those most exquisite arms and legs.
Never before has he loved with such great
passion. But love's beautiful fulfillment
is lacking; the fulfillment is lacking that both of them
ought to have wished for with equal intensity.

(They are both not equally given to this abnormal pleasure.
It totally possesses him only).

And he's wearing down, a complete nervous wreck.
Besides he's out of work, making matters worse.
He manages with difficulty to borrow some
small change (at times
almost begging for it) and lives on the edge.
He kisses the adored lips; pleasures himself
on that exquisite body—even though he feels
now that it merely submits.
And then he drinks and smokes; drinks and smokes;
and drags himself off to the cafés all day,
wearily drags the blight on his beauty.—
"Work with as much as you've got now, mind."

(1928)

In Sparta

King Cleomenes didn't know, didn't dare—
didn't know of any way he could say
this to his mother: Ptolemy was demanding
that as security to their agreement she would
be sent to Egypt, too, and held hostage;
a very humiliating, unseemly thing.
And he kept going on to speak, and kept faltering.
And he kept starting to say something, and always stopped.

But the peerless woman caught on to him
(she'd already heard some rumors about it),
and she encouraged him to speak up.
And she laughed and said she'd certainly go.
And even rejoiced that she could still
be useful to Sparta in her old age.

As for the humiliation—well, she was indifferent to it.
And naturally no Lagid-come-lately
was equipped to grasp the Spartan soul;
so then his demand could not
in fact humiliate a Royal
Lady like her: mother of a Spartan king.

(1928)

Portrait of a Twenty-Three Year Old Painted by His Friend of the Same Age, an Amateur

He finished the portrait   at noon yesterday.
Now he examines it in detail.   He painted him
in an unbuttoned gray jacket,   a deep gray, without
a vest or tie.   With an opened
rose shirt,   to show a little
of his beautiful   chest and neck.
The right side of his forehead   almost entirely
covered with hair,   his lovely hair
(combed in the style   he favors this year).
It's absolutely there   the sensual cast
he wanted to get   when he did the eyes,
when he did the lips ...   That mouth of his, the lips
meant to carry out   choice acts of love.

(1928)

In a Large Greek Colony, 200 B.C.

That things in the Colony aren't going as wished
there can not be any doubt,
and though we somehow push ahead,
perhaps, as more than a few now think, the time has come
for us to bring in a Political Reformer.

But the obstacle and the problem
is that they make such a big deal about
everything, these Reformers.
(What a blessing if one never
needed them). After every little thing,
every detail, they enquire and examine,
and immediately come up with radical modifications,
and demand they be enacted without delay.

They are also partial to sacrifices.
Relinquish that possession of yours;
keeping it is risky business:
it's exactly possessions like those that harm the Colonies.
Relinquish that revenue,
and that other one like it,
and this third one: as a normal consequence.
They are substantial, indeed, but what can be done?
They create a harmful liability for you.

And as they proceed with their audit,
they keep on finding non-essentials, and demand their disposal;
things that are nonetheless hard for one to give up.

And when, in good time, they finish the job,
every single item laid out and precisely pared down,
they depart, taking with them their fair recompense,
now let's see if there's anything left over
after such expert surgery.—

Maybe it isn't time yet.
Let's not make haste; haste is a dangerous thing.
Premature measures bring regret.
For sure and sadly, there's much that's irrational in the Colonies.
But is there anything human without its failings?
And after all, look here, we do push ahead.

(1928)

A Prince from Western Libya

Aristomenes, son of Menelaus,
the prince of Western Libya
was generally well-liked in Alexandria
for the ten days of his sojourn there.
Like his name, his dress, decorous, Greek.
He accepted honors gratefully, but
didn't seek them; he was unassuming.
He bought Greek books,
especially history and philosophy.
Above all he was a man of few words.
He was a deep thinker, it was rumored,
and for such men it was natural to be reticent.

He was neither a deep thinker, nor anything.
An ordinary, ridiculous man.
He took a Greek name, dressed like the Greeks,
learned to carry himself more or less like a Greek,
and his soul shivered in case
he'd spoil his good impression
by speaking Greek with frightful barbarisms,
and the Alexandrians would make fun of him,
as it's their wont to do, terrible people.

That's why he confined himself to a few words,
taking care full of dread with declensions and pronunciation;
and got more than a little bored having
so much conversation piled up inside him.

(1928)

Kimon, Son of Learchus, Age 22, Student of Greek Literature (in Cyrene)

"My end came   at a happy time.
Hermoteles had me   as his inseparable friend.
During my final days,   for all his putting on
that he wasn't worried,   I often sensed
he had been crying.   When he thought
I'd fallen asleep for a bit,   beside himself he'd drop
onto the edge of my bed.   But we were both
young men of the same age,   twenty-three.
Destiny is a cheat.   Maybe another passion
would have taken   Hermoteles away from me.
I ended well: in a love undivided."—

This epitaph   for Marylos, son of Aristodemus,
who died last month   in Alexandria,
I, his cousin Kimon,   received during mourning.
The writer, a poet I know,   sent it to me.
He sent it to me   because he knew
I was related to Marylos: he knew nothing more.
My soul is overrun   with grief for Marylos.
We'd grown up together,   like brothers.
I'm deeply saddened.   His premature death
completely wiped out   any bitterness.....
towards Marylos—   any bitterness, despite
his having stolen Hermoteles'   love from me,
so even if Hermoteles   should want me again now,
it just wouldn't be the same.   I'm well aware of this
delicate temperament of mine.   The image of Marylos
will come between us,   and I'll imagine him
saying, "Look,   you're satisfied now.
Look, you took him back   just as you wanted, Kimon.
Look, you no longer have   reason to speak ill of me."

(1928)

On the March to Sinope

Mithridates, glorious and powerful,
lord of great cities,
commander of mighty armies and fleets,
traveling to Sinope took a rural
road in a remote part of the country
where a soothsayer lived.

Mithridates dispatched an officer
to ask the soothsayer how much more power
and wealth he'd acquire in the future.

He dispatched the officer, and he
continued on his march to Sinope.

The soothsayer withdrew into a secret room.
After about half an hour he emerged
preoccupied, and said to the officer,
"I wasn't able to discern much satisfactorily.
Today is not a propitious day.
I saw some shadowy things. Didn't understand them well.—
The king should be content with what he has.
Anything more will put him in danger.
Remember to tell him this, officer:
for god's sake, let him go on being content with what he has!
Fortune takes sudden turns.
Say this to King Mithridates:
very rarely does one encounter the noble companion
of his ancestor, who wrote with his lance on the ground
just in time to save him, FLEE MITHRIDATES."

(1928)

Days of 1909, '10, and '11

He was the son of a ground down poverty-stricken
sailor (from an island in the Aegean Sea).
He worked for a blacksmith. He wore shabby clothes.
His work shoes were shredded and pitiful.
His hands were grimy with rust and grease.

Evenings, after the shop was closed,
if there was something he really wanted,
like a fairly expensive tie,
like a tie for Sundays,
or if he'd seen and hankered after
a beautiful mauve shirt in a shop window,
he'd sell his body for a shilling or two.

I ask myself if in its olden times
glorious Alexandria could show a youth that lovely,
a boy more perfect than he—who'd gone to waste:
I mean no statue or painting of him was ever done;
hurled into that hideous old blacksmith shop,
in no time the ruinous heavy work
and pedestrian debauchery used him up.

(1928)

Myres: Alexandria, 340 A.D.

When I learned the disastrous news that Myres had died,
I went to his house, although I refrain
from entering Christian homes,
especially at times of mourning or holidays.

I stood in the hall. I didn't want
to go inside any further, because I noticed
that the relatives of the deceased were looking at me
with obvious surprise and annoyance.

They had laid him out in a large room
of which I could see a small part from
the corner where I stood; all expensive carpets
and silver and gold vessels.

I stood in a corner of the hall and wept.
And thought about how our gatherings and excursions
won't amount to much anymore without Myres
and thought about how I would no longer see him
at our lovely and shocking all-nighters
enjoying himself, laughing, and reciting verses
with his expert sense of Greek rhythm;
and thought about how I'd forever lost
his beauty, lost forever
the young man I'd adored to distraction.

Some old women near me were talking with lowered voices
about the last day of his life—
the name of Christ constantly on his lips,
holding a cross in his hands.—
Then four Christian priests entered
the room fervently saying
prayers and entreaties to Jesus,
or to Mary (I don't know their religion well).

Of course, we knew Myres was Christian.
We knew from the very first hour when
he'd come into our crowd year before last.
He lived exactly as we did.
Of all of us the most profligate in pursuit of pleasures;
showering his money extravagantly on amusements.
Careless about other people's opinions,
he threw himself readily into night-time street fights
when that gang of ours happened
to cross paths with a gang of rivals.
We never discussed his religion.
In fact, once we told him
we were taking him with us to the Serapeum.
But he seemed to be offended
by our little joke: I remember it now.
Ah, and now two other occasions come to mind.
When we made libations to Poseidon,
he pulled out of our circle, and looked the other way.
When one of us enthusiastically
said, May our company always come under
the favor and protection of the great,
the supremely beautiful Apollo—Myres whispered
(the others didn't hear) "except for me."

The priests were praying loudly
for the young man's soul.—
I remarked with how much diligence
and with what intense care
for the formalities of their religion, they were preparing
everything for the Christian funeral.
And suddenly a peculiar sensation
overcame me. I had this hazy feeling
that Myres was deserting me;
I had a feeling that he, a Christian, was bonded
to his own people, and that I was becoming
a stranger, a total stranger; I even felt
a doubt overtaking me: possibly I'd been fooled

by my own passion, and had *always* been a stranger.—
I sped out of their hideous house,
quickly left before their Christianity
could tear away, could distort my memory of Myres.

(1929)

Alexander Jannaeus and Alexandra

Successful and completely satisfied,
King Alexander Jannaeus
and his wife Queen Alexandra
pass with musicians in the lead
and with every kind of majesty and opulence,
they pass through the streets of Jerusalem.
It's come to a brilliant fulfillment, the work
begun by the great Judas Maccabeus
and his four illustrious brothers;
and later resolutely continued in the midst
of many dangers and impediments.
Now nothing unbecoming remains.
Every submission to the haughty
monarchs of Antioch has ended. Just see
how King Alexander Jannaeus
and his wife Queen Alexandra
are in all things the equals of the Seleucids.
Good Jews, pure Jews, pious Jews—above all.
But, as circumstances would have it,
also accomplished in speaking Greek;
and on intimate terms with Greeks and Hellenized
monarchs—but as equals, let it be understood.
Indeed, it turned out brilliantly,
It turned out remarkably
the work begun by the great Judas Maccabeus
and his four illustrious brothers.

(1929)

Lovely White Flowers So Well-Suited

He entered the café   where they used go together.—
Three months ago   it was here his friend had told him,
"We're dead broke.   Two down and out boys
we are—reduced   to the cheapest spots.
I'm telling you up front,   I can't keep on going
with you. Someone else,   get it, wants me."
This someone else had promised him   two suits and some
silk handkerchiefs.—   To get him back he turned
the world upside down   and came up with twenty pounds.
He went back to him   for the twenty pounds;
but along with all that,   for their old attachment,
for their old love,   for the deep feeling between them.—
That "someone else" was a liar,   a real low-life;
he'd had only one suit   made for him, and
that under constraint,   with a thousand pleas.

But now he wants   neither suits,
nor silk handkerchiefs   any longer, any way,
nor twenty pounds,   or even twenty piastres.

Sunday they buried him,   at ten in the morning.
Sunday they buried him: it's been almost a week.

On his inexpensive coffin   he laid flowers,
lovely white flowers   so well-suited
to his beauty and   his twenty-three years.

When he went that evening—   it happened he had business
essential to his bread and butter—   to the café they
used to go together: a knife to the heart
that sad café   where they used to go together.

(1929)

Come, O King of the Lacedaimonians

Cratisicleia did not deign to allow
the people to see her weeping and grieving;
she walked in stately silence.
Her serene demeanor revealed
nothing of her sorrow and her torments.
But even so, for a moment she couldn't contain herself;
and before she boarded the hateful ship for Alexandria,
she took her son to Poseidon's temple,
and when they were alone she embraced him
and kissed him, who was "suffering grievous pain," says
Plutarch, "in a state of conturbation."
But her strong character fought back;
and regaining her self-composure, the magnificent woman
said to Cleomenes, "Come, O King of the
Lacedaimonians, when we come out
of here, let no one see us weeping
or acting in any way unworthy
of Sparta. For this alone is in our power;
our fortune will be only what the god might give."

And she boarded the ship, heading for that "might give."

(1929)

In the Same Space

Surroundings of home, coffeehouses, the neighborhood
that I have seen and walked year after year.

I created you in happiness and in sorrow:
with so much occurring, under so many conditions.

And you have become a sum-total of feeling for me.

(1929)

The Mirror in the Vestibule

The grand house had in its vestibule
a colossal, extremely old mirror,
bought at least eighty years ago.

A very handsome boy, a tailor's helper
(on Sundays an amateur athlete),
stood there with a package. He gave it
to a member of the household, who took it in
to bring back the receipt. The tailor's helper
was left alone, and waited.
He approached the mirror, looked at himself,
and straightened his tie. After five minutes
they brought him the receipt. He took it and left.

But the old mirror that had seen so much
during the long years of its existence,
thousands of things and faces,
that old mirror was now overjoyed,
and filled with pride at having taken on
perfect beauty for a few moments.

(1930)

He Asked about the Quality

He stepped out of the office where he'd been hired
in a routine, low-paying position
(up to eight pounds a month, with gratuities)
having finished the poor excuse for a job
he'd hunched over all afternoon:
he stepped out at seven, walking slowly
and dallying down the street. —Handsome,
interesting: in his way showing he'd reached
the height of his sensual power.
He had turned twenty-nine the month before.

He dallied down the street and the seedy
side streets that led to his place.

Passing in front of a small shop
that specialized in selling cheap
and shoddy goods for the working class,
he saw a face inside, he saw a form
that drove him to go in and pretend
an interest in some colored neckerchiefs.

He asked about the quality of the neckerchiefs
and their price in a choked voice,
almost smothered by desire,
and the answers came back in the same way,
vague, in a lowered voice,
implying consent.

They kept on talking about the items—but
with a single purpose: to touch hands
over the neckerchiefs, to bring close
their faces, their lips, as if by chance:
a moment's contact of their limbs.

Quickly, surreptitiously, so the shopkeeper
sitting in the back wouldn't catch on.

(1930)

Should Have Taken Care

I'm almost down to being a homeless beggar.
This fatal city, Antioch
has devoured all my assets:
this fatal city with its exorbitant life-style.

But I'm young and in the best of health.
Admirably fluent in Greek
(I know Aristotle and Plato inside and out;
your orators, your poets, you name them).
I'm reasonably familiar with military affairs,
and am friendly with the mercenary commanders.
I'm also somewhat connected in the administration.
Last year I spent six months in Alexandria;
I've a handle (and this is useful) on what goes on there:
the Malefactor's schemes and villainies, et cetera.

So I regard myself as fully
qualified to serve this country,
my beloved homeland, Syria.

In whatever job they give me I'll try
to be helpful to the country. That's my intention.
But if they frustrate me with their usual numbers—
we know who those do-gooders are: enough said;
if they frustrate me, I'm not to blame.

First, I'll apply to Zabinas,
and if that moron doesn't appreciate me,
I'll go to his competitor, Grypus.
And if that idiot doesn't appoint me,
I'll go straight to Hyrcanus.

In any case, one of those three will want me.

And I have a clear conscience
about my indifference to the choice.
All three are equally harmful to Syria.

But, wreck of a man that I am, I'm not to blame.
Miserable wretch, I'm just trying to patch up my life.
Had the almighty gods cared
to create a fourth, good man.
I'd have happily gone with him.

(1930)

According to the Recipes of Ancient Greco-Syrian Magicians

"What distillate of magic herbs
can I find," said an aesthete,
"what distillate according to the recipes
of ancient Greco-Syrian magicians
that for a day (if its power
won't last longer) or for just a moment
might bring back my age of twenty-three,
my friend of twenty-two,
bring back—his beauty and his love.

"What distillate can I find according to the recipes
of ancient Greco-Syrian magicians
that, in keeping with this return to the past,
might bring back our little room."

(1931)

In the Year 200 B.C.

"Alexander, son of Philip, and the Greeks
except the Lacedaimonians..."

We can indeed imagine
the utterly unsympathetic response in Sparta
to this inscription. "Except for the Lacedaimonians,"
naturally. It was not for the Spartans
to be led and ordered about
like prized servants. Moreover
a panhellenic campaign without
a Spartan king as its leader
would not have seemed very special to them.
But of course, "except the Lacedaimonians."

That's one way of looking at it. Good enough.

Thus, minus the Lacedaimonians at Granikos,
and at Issus, then at the decisive
battle where the fearsome army
the Persians raised at Arbela was crushed:
it mobilized from Arbela for victory and was crushed.

And from this fabulous panhellenic campaign,
so victorious, so brilliant,
renowned and glorified
as none other had been glorified,
peerless, we emerged:
a new and great Hellenic world.

We, the Alexandrians, the Antiochians,
the Seleucians, and the numerous
other Greeks of Egypt and Syria,
and those in Media and Persia, and all the rest.
With our vast dominion,
our diverse powers of well-planned accommodation,

and our new Greek Vernacular
which carries as far as Bactria, to the Indians.

Talk about Lacedaimonians now!

(1931)

Days of 1908

That year he found himself out of work,
and so he lived off of card games,
backgammon, and loans.

He was offered a job at a small
stationery store at three pounds a month.
But he didn't hesitate at all to turn it down.
It wouldn't do. It was not a salary for him,
a fairly well educated young man of twenty-five.

Some days he won two or three shillings, others none.
What could the boy make out of cards and backgammon
in the working-class cafés of his social level,
no matter how smartly he played, or picked dense opponents?
As for his loans, they scarcely broke even.
He rarely came up with a crown, usually half,
at times came down to a shilling.

For a week, sometimes longer,
when he escaped the hideous all-nighters,
he refreshed himself at the baths, with a morning swim.

His clothes were in a terribly sad state.
He always wore the same suit, a suit
of extremely faded cinnamon color.

O summer days of nineteen hundred and eight,
from your view, in the best of taste,
the faded cinnamon colored suit is missing.

Your view has preserved him
as he was when he removed them, threw them off,
those unfit clothes and mended underwear,
and stood stark naked, perfectly handsome, a miracle,
with his uncombed hair swept back,

with his limbs lightly tanned
from his morning nakedness at the baths and on the beach.

(1932)

In the Outskirts of Antioch

We in Antioch were floored when we heard
about Julian's latest number.

Apollo had explained himself clearly at Daphne!
He didn't want to offer an oracle (we should give a damn!),
didn't mean to speak prophetically, until
his temple in Daphne was purified.
He was annoyed, he stated, by the neighboring dead.

There are many tombs in Daphne.—
One of those buried there
was the prodigious, the glory of our church,
the holy and triumphant martyr, Vavylas.

It was him the false god intimated, him he feared.
As long as he sensed his presence, he didn't dare
turn out an oracle--mum's the word.
(The false gods tremble before our martyrs.)

The impious Julian rolled up his sleeves,
got mad and shouted: "Dig him up, take him away,
get rid of this Vavylas right away.
Do you hear? He annoys Apollo.
Dig him up, deal with him at once.
Disinter him, take him wherever you want.
Get him out, throw him out. Think we're playing a game?
Apollo said the temple must be purified."

We took it up, we carried the holy relic elsewhere.
We took it up, we carried it in love and honor.

And the temple has done real well.
In no time, there was a fire,
a big blazing awful fire.
And both Apollo and temple burned down.

Idol to ashes: to be dumped with the trash.

Julian just lost it and put out the word—
what else could he do?—that the fire had been set
by us Christians. Let him say so.
He's got no proof. Let him say so.
The main thing is, he just lost it.

(1933)

Notes

'Achilles' Horses' (p.34)
Their names were Xanthus and Balius. See the *Iliad*, XVI. 145-54 and XVII. 423-49. This poem, 'Sarpedon's Funeral,' 'Interruption,' 'Perfidy,' and 'Trojans' share in a common Homeric and mythological background.

'Sarpedon's Funeral' (p.36)
See the *Iliad*, XVI. 462-675.

'The First Step' (p.39)
Theokritos, the great pastoral poet, was probably born circa 300 B.C. in the Sicilian Greek city of Syracuse, though some authorities believe his birthplace was the island of Kos. The scene of the poem is usually identified as Syracuse, but I believe Cavafy may have had in mind Alexandria, where Theokritos spent a good part of his career.

'Che Fece... Il Gran Rifuto' (p.41)
See Dante, *Inferno*, III. 60.

'Interruption' (p.42)
See *The Homeric Hymn to Demeter*, 230-74 and Apollodorus, *The Library*, III. xiii, 5-6.

'Thermoplyae' (p.44)
The title refers to the famous battle in 480 B.C. in the mountainous pass defended by the Greeks under the command of the Spartan king Leonidas against the invading Medes, i.e., Persians. Ephialtes was a traitorous local Greek who led the Persians to a footpath that enabled them to attack the Greek forces from the rear.

'King Demetrius' (p.54)
In 288 B.C., Demetrius the Besieger, king of Macedonia, was abandoned by his forces, which went over to the side of the invading Pyrrhus, king of Epirus.

'The Footsteps' (p.58)
See Suetonius, *The Life of Nero*, 46. The Furies pursued Nero for the sin of matricide.

'He's the Man' (p.59)
See *The Dream*, 11, by Lucian of Samosata (c. 120–c.180 A.D.) in which the allegorical figure Culture, or Education (*Paideia* in Greek), vying with Craft (*Techne*) for the narrator's favor, promises him fame in return for his service.

The Edessene poet is from Edessa, the capital of the Mesopotamian kingdom of Osroene.

'The Satrapy' (p.61)
The Persian Empire was divided into provinces called *satrapies*. Susa was the capital of Persia during its early history.

'The Ides of March' (p.62)
March 15, 44 B.C. was the day on which Julius Caesar was assassinated despite the effort of his friend, the Greek philosopher Artemidorus, to warn him.

'Sculptor from Tyana' (p.64)
Tyana was a city in Cappadocia, Asia Minor. The sculptor's subjects cover a familiar range of conventional mythological and historical figures. On Caesarion, see the note on the poem of that name below.

'The God Abandons Antony' (p.65)
The title of this poem comes from the end of a passage in Plutarch's *Life of Antony*, 75.3-4, in which a Bacchic procession is described as passing through the city and departing it from the gate that faced Antony and Cleopatra's enemies. This was interpreted as a sign that Antony's favorite god, Dionysus, had abandoned him.

'The Glory of the Ptolemies' (p.67)
The Ptolemies refers to the dynasty of Egyptian kings and queens descended from Alexander the Great's general Ptolemy. Seleucid refers to the dynastic royal line of Syria. The city, of course, is Alexandria.

'Ithaca' (p.68)
The title of this poem, which denotes the island home of Odysseus, is the first of four explicit references to Homer's *Odyssey*, the epic about the hero's return to his homeland after the victory at Troy. The other references are to three of the hero's numerous adversaries who attempted to prevent his homecoming: the Laestrygonians were giant cannibals who devoured foreigners, the Cyclopes were savage one-eyed giants, the most brutish of which was Polyphemus, whom Odysseus blinded, thereby earning the wrath of his father Poseidon, god of the sea.

'Dangerous Matters' (p.70)
Constans and Constantius were two of three sons, the third being Constantine II, among whom the emperor Constantine the Great divided the Roman Empire after his death; their joint rule extended from 337 to 351 A.D.

'Philhellene' (p.71)
Zagros is the name of a mountain range in Asia Minor. Phraata was a city in Media.

'Herodes Atticus' (p.72)
Herodes Atticus (101–177 A.D.) was the most famous and prosperous of the second-century sophists. The sophist Alexander was nicknamed "the Clay Plato" by Philostratus in his *The Lives of the Sophists*. For an enlightening account of this period in Greek cultural and literary history, see Tim Whitmarsh, *The Second Sophistic*, Cambridge University Press, 2005.

'Alexandrian Kings' (p.73)
The royal spectacle described in this poem was personally staged by Marc Antony. Also see the poem 'Caesarion.'

'Theodotus' (p.87)
Although history credits the rhetorician Theodotus with having convinced the Egyptians to murder Pompey in 48 B.C., there is no record of his actually delivering his head to Caesar.

'Orophernes' (p.93)
Orophernes' mother, Antiochis, daughter of Antiochus III the Great of Syria, alleged his father was Ariarathes of Cappadocia. His grandmother, Stratonice, was the daughter of Antiochus II. Demetrius of Syria (see 'The Displeasure of the Seleucid' and 'Of Demetrius Soter (162–150 B.C.)' made him king of Cappadocia in 157 B. C., but he was deposed three years later. Given refuge in Antioch, Orophernes responded by plotting to usurp the throne of his protector.

'The Battle of Magnesia' (p.95)
Cavafy imagines how Philip V of Macedon, seven years after being abandoned by his allies and defeated by the Romans in 197 B.C., received the news of the defeat of Antiochus III of Syria by the Romans at Magnesia (see 'Craftsman of Wine Bowls').

'Manuel Comnenus' (p.96)
Manuel Comnenus I (1118–1180) ruled the Byzantine Empire from 1143 until the day of his death on September 24, 1180. His reign began with glorious success and came to a close in a state of shattering defeat.

'The Displeasure of the Seleucid' (p.97)
The historical principals of this drama are Demetrius of Syria and Ptolemy VI of Egypt when both were in Rome in 164 B.C. Demetrius was a political hostage waiting for the opportune time to ascend to the throne of Syria as Soter (the

Savior); and Ptolemy VI, after having been expelled from Egypt by his younger brother Ptolemy VIII, had come to beg the Romans to support his reinstatement.

'Facing the Statue of Endymion' (p.100)
In a Greek myth, Selene, the Moon, saw a beautiful young shepherd named Endymion and fell madly in love with him. In one version, Selene asked Zeus to grant the youth a single wish, and he chose eternal sleep in his beauteous, ageless state; in another, Selene saw him in this sleep and fell in love with him. One of his graves was supposed to have been on Mount Latmus in Asia Minor.

'In a Town in Osroene' (p.101)
Osroene, was an ancient kingdom in northwest Mesopotamia (present day southeast Turkey and northeast Syria). Charmides was Plato's uncle, after whom the philosopher named one of his dialogues, in which the young Charmides is described as "a marvel of stature and beauty" (154c).

'Gray' (p.107)
Two of the better known and more frequently cited volumes of Cavafy translations, those by Edmund Keeley and Philip Sherrard (*C. P. Cavafy, Collected Poems*, Princeton University Press, 1975) and by Daniel Mendelsohn (*C. P. Cavafy, Collected Poems*, Alfred A. Knopf, 2009) make the same point, though in very different ways, in their annotations to this poem. According to Keeley and Sherrard, "In the original, the sex of the person with the gray eyes remains ambiguous." According to Mendelsohn, "Cavafy takes conspicuous pains to conceal the sex of the beloved in this poem: in the Greek, no pronoun is given as the subject of either of the two active verbs—'departs' in line 5, 'lives' in line 7. I have rendered these lines so as to preserve this important ambiguity." Keeley and Sherrard translate the verbs with the subject "he," as they should. ("Then he went away to work" and "Those gray eyes will have lost their charm—if he's still alive;"). Mendelsohn, in order to sustain the hidden identity of the beloved's gender in his translation, which he seems to believe is literally indispensible to the poem's integrity, takes, in turn, conspicuous pains to override the literal sense of the poem's language in order to satisfy his need for fidelity by changing the verb "departs" to a noun in "Then the departure" and the verb phrase "if (subject understood) lives" to "if they're alive" by switching the subject of the verb's agreement from the individual to his/ her/ or its eyes, ("Those gray eyes— if they're alive—will have lost their beauty;"). There are, of course, other poems in which the gender of the desired is not explicit, as, for example, in 'Faraway,' 'Days of 1903,' and 'Half an Hour,' none of which are so annotated in these two editions (though Keeley and Sherrard categorize all five poems whose titles begin 'Days of…' as being "obviously related to Cavafy's 'secret life'"), probably because such an awareness should and does not affect the translation process. A striking difference occurs with the poem 'The Afternoon Sun,' however, where

the sex ambiguity is dutifully noted by Keeley and Sherrard and dealt with once again by translating the Greek verb-without-a-pronoun "wrote" in the only way they should, "In the middle the table where he wrote." Mendelsohn demurs from noting anything here concerning the previously described instance of same sex ambiguity in 'Gray,' and appears either to have changed his mind about his former stand, possibly finding the ambiguity insufficiently compelling, or simply forgot about it because this time he translates the line as he should, "In the middle, the table where he'd write," a pronounced improvement over attempts at more resourceful renderings. But then comes the poem just a couple of pages away, 'The Next Table,' whose note and translation of the three verbs describing the state of being and acts of the beloved Keeley and Sherrard treat in their usual way, as does Mendelsohn ("As in 'Gray,' Cavafy's Greek makes it impossible to determine the gender of the object of the speaker's desire.") and proceeds to cut the pronoun "he" from the verb "must be" at the very beginning of the poem by substituting the negative construction "Can't be more than twenty-two years old," then in the final stanza cuts the pronoun again from "[he's] sitting," and, depriving the desired object of [his] motor abilities and the poem of its most graphic moment, removes the active verb altogether with the verging on solipsistic, "I recognize each movement." There is a way, perhaps more than one, in which difference from the pack may be asserted, and in this case it may be said almost all other translators of Cavafy honor the effect of the verb by supplying its implied pronoun subject, an outcome, if I may be allowed a moment of subjectivity, I can readily imagine the poet of 'Hidden Things' anticipating. And besides, the contextual venues of these poems, the setting of a casino in 'The Next Table,' for example, introduce a countervailing case for the perception of masculine sexual identity against one for airtight ambiguity of gender.

'In the Month of Athyr' (p.109)
Athyr, the third month of the Egyptian calendar, corresponding to our October-November, was named after the goddess of sensual love and tombs. Kappa Zeta in Greek numerals stands for 27.

'Symeon' (p.115)
The poem's title refers to the Syrian Saint Symeon Stylites (Greek for "of the pillar"), who died c. 459 A.D. Libanios (314–c. 393) was a well-known Syrian rhetorician of the time. Meleagros, a renowned Greek poet who also made an important collection of poems that became the nucleus of the famous *Greek Anthology*, was born in Gadara, Syria, c. 140 B.C.

'Caesarion' (p.116)
Caesarion was the nickname Marc Antony gave to Ptolemy XV, the son of Julius Caesar and Cleopatra (see 'Alexandrian Kings'). In 31 B.C., Octavian (Augustus) ordered the execution of Caesarion after the Roman victory at Actium and the subsequent suicides of Antony and Cleopatra. For the Homeric source of

Octavian's advisors' wordplay in the poem's last line, see the *Iliad*, II. 204.

'Nero's Deadline' (p.120)
Galba, Roman general and governor of Spain, was asked to replace Nero in 68 A.D. He succeeded him as emperor at the age of seventy-three. See Suetonius. *The Life of Nero*, 40.

'Envoys from Alexandria' (p.121)
Though this complex consultation of the oracle at Delphi is imaginary, the quarrel between these two brothers and its Roman resolution was real enough. See 'The Displeasure of the Seleucid.'

'Aristoboulus' (p.122)
At the age of seventeen, Aristoboulus, a Hasmonean and brother of Herod I the Great's wife Miriam, had been appointed high priest by Herod at the insistence of his mother-in-law Alexandra. A year later in 35 B.C., Herod wanted him out of the way and ordered him drowned ("make it look like an accident"). He was urged to do this by his mother Cypris and his infamous sister Salome, about whom Cavafy wrote but never published the following poem in 1896:

> *Salome*
>
> Enter Salome, with John the Baptist's
> head upon a charger. The young Greek
> *rhetor* leaning, indifferently, away from love,
> couldn't be bothered less.
>
> "I do wish, instead," he responds
> "they'd serve me your head upon this."
> He had his way of ribbing her, until
> a runner slave of hers, on the next day,
>
> comes in holding his lover's blonde-tressed
> head upon a golden tray.
> Our *rhetor* was so engrossed in study he forgot
> the wish he had expressed the previous day.
>
> The splatter so revolts him now he orders
> the bleedy mess to be removed
> from sight, then turns once more
> to reading the dialogues of Plato.
>
> *(Translation by Stavros Deligiorgis)*

'Imenus' (p.132)
Michael the Third, also known as "the drunkard," was Byzantine Emperor from 842 to 867 A. D.

'Of Demetrius Soter (162–150 B.C.)' (p.134)
See 'The Displeasure of the Seleucid.' After escaping from Rome and recovering the throne of Syria in 162 B.C., Demetrius was eventually defeated and killed in 150 B.C. by the pretender to the throne Alexander Valas (see 'The Favor of Alexander Valas'). Five years later, Valas was overthrown in a plot led by Herakleides (see 'Craftsman of Wine Bowls'), a former satrap of Babylon.

'If Dead Then' (p.137)
This poem's title comes from Philostratus' famous biographical work *In Honor of Apollonius of Tyana*, VIII. 29 (c. 220 A.D.), on which and on whose proper title see Whitmarsh, *The Second Sophistic*, pp. 76-77. Philostratus' work, as indicated by the poem's speaker, who supposedly lived during the reign of the Byzantine emperor Justin I (518–527 A.D.), was alleged to have been based on the account by Damis, one of Apollonius' students. Dictynna, also known as Britomartis, was a Minoan goddess. See also the poems, 'But Wise Men Apprehend What Is Imminent' and 'Apollonius of Tyana in Rhodes.'

'Young Men of Sidon (400 A.D.)' (p.139)
Sidon, on the site of present-day Sayda, Lebanon, was a prosperous port city of Phoenicia. For Meleagros, see the note above on 'Symeon.' Minor poet and erotic epigrammatist Krinagoras (first century B.C.) of Mytilene on the island of Lesbos, served as an ambassador to Julius Caesar in Rome and to Augustus Caesar in Spain. Rhianos (circa 200 B.C.) was probably a slave from Crete who wrote epic poetry and edited Homer as well as composing some epigrams. The great dramatist Aeschylus (525–456 B.C.) supposedly wrote or ordered his own epitaph, parts of which are quoted in the poem, in which he sought to preserve only the memory of what the man had done at Marathon because he was fully confident in the undying power of what the poet had accomplished in Athens. Datis and Artaphernes, a nephew of Darius, led the Persian force that was defeated by the Athenians, with Aeschylus in their ranks, at the Battle of Marathon in 490 B.C.

'Darius' (p.141)
Darius (521–486 B. C.), one of the Persia's greatest kings, is best known for his invasion of Greece and defeat at Marathon in 490 B.C. Mithridates VI Eupator was the Persian king of Pontos (120–63 B.C.). Amissos was a city on the Black Sea, which the Romans took in 71 B.C.

'Anna Comnena' (p.143)
Anna Comnena (1083-1146) was the daughter of the Byzantine emperor Alexius I Comnenus, about whom she wrote her poem the *Alexiad* after her retirement to a monastery following her failure to outmaneuver her brother John II for the succession in behalf of her husband. The quotations in the second stanza come from the beginning of her poem.

'A Byzantine Noble in Exile, Versifying' (p.144)
The Byzantine emperor Nicephorus III Botaniates deposed Michael VII in 1078 and was himself dethroned three years later by Alexius Comnenus, husband of Irene Ducas and father of Anna Comnena.

'The Favor of Alexander Valas' (p.146)
Alexander Valas was the king of Syria (150–145 B.C.). See 'Of Demetrius Soter (162–150 B.C.).'

'Melancholy of Jason Cleander, Poet in Commagene, 595 A.D.' (p.147)
Commagene, once a territory within the kingdom of Syria, was part of the Byzantine Empire until 638 A.D., when it was conquered by the Arabs.

'Demaratus' (p.148)
The reference to Porphyry (234–c. 305 A.D.) points to a late third/ early fourth century for this imaginary essayist (the suggestion that the name may not refer to the famous Neoplatonist but merely to some individual who happens to be named Porphyry because philosophers don't bother with students not only begs the question but also proposes a quirky practice that is not consistent with Cavafy's poetic character). Demaratus, King of Sparta (510–491 B.C.), ruled jointly with Kleomenes I, who, with the help of Leotychides, bribed the Delphic Oracle to deny Demaratus was the legitimate son of King Ariston. Demaratus fled to the Persian court of Darius and subsequently accompanied Xerxes on his catastrophic campaign against Greece, in which Leotychides played an important role as commander of the Greek fleet.

'From the School of the Renowned Philosopher' (p.151)
Ammonius Saccas, who died in 243 A.D., taught in Alexandria where he was known as the 'Socrates of Neoplatonism.' Though no writings of his survive, such famous individuals as Plotinus, Longinus, and Origen were numbered among his students.

'Craftsman of Wine Bowls' (p.152)
In 190 B.C., the Romans defeated Antiochos III at Magnesia, in Lydia, an event that confirmed their supremacy in the East.

'Those Who Fought for the Achaean League' (p.153)
As the closing couplet indicates, this epigram was supposedly composed in 109 B.C. during the undistinguished reign of Ptolemy IX (116–80 B.C.), nicknamed "the Chickpea" (Lathyros). The Achaean League (280–146 B.C.), a confederation of mainland Greeks to oppose the Romans, came to an end when its forces, under the command of Diaeus and Critolaus, were defeated at Corinth by the Romans in 146.

'To Antiochus Epiphanes' (p.154)
Antiochus IV Epiphanes, who reigned in Syria from 175 to 169 B.C., was the son of Antiochus III the Great, whom the Romans defeated at the Battle of Magnesia in 190 B.C. The Macedonian effort to undo Roman domination came to an end at the Battle of Pydna in 168 B.C.

'Julian Seeing Indifference' (p.157)
Julian, Roman Emperor from 361–63 A.D., was a nephew of Constantine the Great and originally a Christian, but when he renounced his religion and converted to paganism he earned the epithet "the Apostate." The quotation with which the poem begins is from a letter of appointment written in 363 to Theodorus as High Priest of Asia. See the following related poems: 'Julian in Nicomedia,' 'A Great Procession of Priests and Laymen,' 'Julian and the Antiochians,' 'You Didn't Understand,' and 'On the Outskirts of Antioch.'

'Epitaph of Antiochus, King of Commagene' (p.158)
Antiochus IV Epiphanes, who ruled from 175 to 163 B.C., was the son of Antiochus III the Great of Syria.

'Julian in Nicomedia' (p.160)
In 351 A.D. at the age of twenty, ten years before he became emperor, Julian was living in Nicomedia, the capital of Bithynia in Asia Minor, trying to conceal his growing interest in paganism. The neoplatonists Chrysanthius and Maximus of Ephesus were two of his influential teachers, the latter especially in the subject of theurgy. Mardonius was his long-time tutor. Gallus, Julian's Christian half-brother, was executed by the Emperor Constantius II, also a Christian, in 354.

'31 B.C. in Alexandria' (p.163)
After Octavius, soon to be Caesar Augustus, thoroughly defeated the forces of Marc Antony and Cleopatra in the Battle of Actium in 31 B.C., the resourceful queen staged a triumphant return to Alexandria in order to hide the disastrous news from her subjects.

'John Cantacuzenus Triumphs' (p.164)
Having been appointed regent in 1341 A.D. upon the death of Byzantine Emperor Andronicus III Palaeologos, whose son John was but nine years of age

at the time, John Cantacuzenus (c. 1292–1383) was challenged by Andronicus' widow Anna of Savoy and her powerful allies despite the fact that John had pledged to remain as regent and guardian to the young heir until he came of age. In response, "the Reluctant Emperor," as John was known, proclaimed himself emperor, and successfully put down the attempted coup. See the poem 'Of Colored Glass' below on his coronation and that of his wife Irene. In 1354, he abdicated and became a monk.

'Temethus, Antiochian: 400 A.D.' (p.165)
Samosata was the capital of Commagene, a small state in Syria. The hundred thirty-seventh year "of the Greek reign" would be 175 B.C., following the founding of the Seleucid dynasty in 312 B.C.

'Of Colored Glass' (p.166)
See 'John Cantacuzenus Triumphs.' The coronations of John VI (1347–54) and of his wife Irene, who was related to the imperial family, had to be held in the Blachernae Palace rather than in Haghia Sofia, which was in a damaged state as a result of the struggle with Anna and her supporters. The conflict had left Constantinople and the empire in an impoverished condition.

'On an Italian Shore' (p.168)
It is 146 B.C., the year in which the Roman general Mummius sacked and burned Corinth, slaughtered the men, enslaved the women and children, and brought home the loot. See 'Those Who Fought for the Achaean League.'

'Apollonius of Tyana in Rhodes' (p.170)
See 'If Dead Then.' The quotation is from Philostratus' *In Honor of Apollonius of Tyana*, V. 22.

'In a Township in Asia Minor' (p.172)
The quoted document is fictional. On the battle of Actium, see '31 B.C. in Alexandria.'

'Priest at the Serapeum' (p.173)
The Serapeum of Alexandria, a magnificent temple dedicated to the worship of Serapis, a syncretic Hellenistic and Egyptian god combining features of Osiris and Apis, was built by Ptolemy I c. 300 B.C. and destroyed by the Christian Byzantine emperor Theodosius in 391 A.D.

'A Great Procession of Priests and Laymen' (p.175)
Julian died in June of 363 A.D. at the age of thirty-one as a result of wounds sustained in battle with the Persians. Jovian, a Christian who served in the same campaign, succeeded him as emperor but died several months later.

'Julian and the Antiochians' (p.177)
The epigraph is from a satirical work by Julian in which he pokes a little fun at himself but mostly attacks the Christian city of Antioch for rejecting him and his efforts to restore paganism. According to Julian as he continues, following the quoted passage, the Chi (Christ) was a weak, inefficient god, and the Kappa (Constantius, Julian's predecessor) was not only avaricious and neglectful of the city's pagan glories, but had also harmed the Antiochians by not putting him to death when he had the chance.

'Anna Dalassene' (p.178)
When the Byzantine emperor Alexius Comnenus departed on a military campaign in 1091, he turned over the affairs of state to his mother, Anna Dalassene (1025–1102), naming her Regent. The last line of the poem is a quotation from her grand-daughter's epic poem the *Alexiad*. See 'Anna Comnena.'

'Greek Since Ancient Times' (p.182)
Ione, a town named after the mythical figure Io, was the ancient site of Antioch, which was founded by Seleucus I Nicator in 300 B.C.

'You Didn't Understand' (p.184)
The quotation, from the *Ecclesiastical History*, V. 18 by Sozomenus (c. 400–c. 450 B.C.), records a play on words by Julian, *anegnon, egnon, kategnon*, to which the Christians replied in kind with a clever play on words of their own.

'In Sparta' (p.186)
Cleomenes III of Sparta, who reigned from 235 to 219 B.C., having requested aid from Ptolemy III, the king of Egypt, in his war against Macedonia and the Achaean league, was required to send his children and his mother Cratisicleia to Alexandria as hostages in return for Egyptian support. This poem and the poem 'Come, O King of the Lacedaimonians' are drawn from Plutarch's *Life of Agis and Cleomenes*, 22. 3-8.

'On the March to Sinope' (p.192)
Six kings of Pontus were named Mithridates. This poem is probably about Mithridates V, who was murdered by his wife in Sinope in 120 B.C. The imagined visit to the soothsayer refers to the saving of one of his royal ancestors by Demetrius of Macedonia (337–283 B.C.). See the poem 'King Demetrius.'

'Alexander Jannaeus and Alexandra' (p.197)
Alexander Jannaeus, a Hasmonean who reigned as king of Judea from 103 to 76 B.C., was descended from the Maccabees, whose revolt against the Seleucids in 142 initiated an eighty-year period of Jewish autonomy. His queen, Alexandra-Salome, was the widow of his brother Aristoboulus I. Her granddaughter was the Alexandra who is mentioned in the poem 'Aristoboulus.'

'Come, O King of the Lacedaimonians' (p.199)
See 'In Sparta.' Cratisicleia's speech, the first words of which serve as the poem's title, is a quotation from Plutarch's *Life of Agis and Cleomenes*, 22, 6. That "might give" eventually turned out to be execution for Cratisicleia and her grandchildren by Ptolemy's successor Ptolemy IV. See Plutrarch's *Life of Agis and Cleomenes*, 38. 4-9.

'Should Have Taken Care' (p.204)
The time of this imaginary situation is the middle 120s B.C. Malefactor (Kakergetes) was a nickname of Ptolemy VIII, who was also called Fatso (Physcon, literally the Bladder). His son Ptolemy IX was nicknamed Chickpea. Zabinas (the Slave) refers to Alexander, the alleged son of Alexander Valas, the pretender to the throne of Syria who was killed by Antiochus VIII Grypus (Hook-nose). John Hyrcanus was the son of Simon Maccabee, king of Judea and father of Alexander Jannaeus. See the poems 'Envoys from Alexandria,' 'Those Who Fought for the Achaean League,' 'Of Demetrius Soter (162–150 B.C.),' 'The Favor of Alexander Valas,' and 'Alexander Jannaeus and Alexandra.'

'In the Year 200 B.C.' (p.207)
The year 200 B.C. sets the poem's point of view 130 years after Alexander the Great's Persian triumphs and just a few years before the Roman conquest of the "new and great Hellenic world" mentioned later in the poem. Lacedaimonians, another name for Spartans, appears in the poem's first line, which is a partial quote from the dedicatory inscription Alexander sent to Athens with the plunder he won at his victories in Persia. Granikos, Issus, and Arbela were major battles in Alexander's Persian campaign. Bactria, situated in present-day northern Afghanistan and southern Uzbekistan, was a Persian satrapy, or province.

'In the Outskirts of Antioch' (p.211)
Daphne was a suburb of Antioch, which Julian visited in 362. Vavylas was Bishop of Antioch from 237 to 250.

Biographical Notes

George Economou was born in Great Falls, Montana, and was educated at Colgate and Columbia Universities. Named twice as Fellow in Poetry by the National Endowment for the Humanities, he has also held fellowships from the Rockefeller Foundation and the American Council of Learned Societies. He taught for twenty-four years in New York City primarily at the Brooklyn Center of Long Island University and also at Wagner College, Hunter College, and Columbia. He retired as Professor Emeritus of English after seventeen years on the faculty of the University of Oklahoma and now lives with his wife, poet-playwright Rochelle Owens, in Philadelphia and Wellfleet, Massachusetts.

Stavros Deligiorgis was born in Sulina, Romania, and was educated at the National University of Athens, Greece, Yale University and the University of California at Berkeley. Twice a fellow at the Center for Advanced Study of the University of Illinois, Champaign-Urbana, he also held a two-year Fulbright research professorships at the University of Bucharest. He taught at the Scuola Superiore Traduttori-Interpreti, Trieste, Italy, and in the Graduate Program of Translation Studies at the University of Athens, Greece. Deligiorgis served on the Ministry of Culture Jury for the Annual Awards for Literary Translation. He retired as Professor Emeritus of English and Comparative Literature after thirty-one years at the University of Iowa. He now lives in Athens and Christendom (as Thos Wyatt would have said).

Pantoum for C. P. Cavafy and a Translator

A task reserved for some mighty king of art,
for himself to find the most fitting language.
He'd be a poet for future generations,
his work never buried inside libraries.

For himself to find the most fitting language
in another is a task intended for a friend,
for work never buried inside libraries
gains a breath of afterlife from that touch.

To another was this task extended as a friend
who'd set it reaching for its fame and to
gain a breath of afterlife from that touch
as it passes from the once and future poet's lips.

He who set it reaching for its fame and
he who found it in a source of grandeur,
pass joined as once and future poets at the lip,
and together say, "Ionia, you own me, Ionia."

He who found it in a source of grandeur,
he'd be a poet for future generations,
and will always say, "Ionia, you own me, Ionia,"
in the task reserved for some mighty king of art.

George Economou

www.ingramcontent.com/pod-product-compliance
Lightning Source LLC
Chambersburg PA
CBHW032127160426
43197CB00008B/547